ECONOMICS OF GROUND WATER MANAGEMENT IN INDIA

ECONOMICS OF GROUND WATER MANAGEMENT IN INDIA

Dr. S. ASAITHAMBI

ABHIJEET PUBLICATIONS

DELHI 110094

ABHIJEET PUBLICATIONS
2/46 Tukhmeerpur Extension
Delhi-110 094
Phone: 011-22960492 (Fax), 65698474
E-mail: abhijeetpublication@gmail.com

ECONOMICS OF GROUND WATER MANAGEMENT IN INDIA

First Published 2008

ISBN 978-81-89886-77-6

PRINTED IN INDIA

Published by J.K. Singh for Abhijeet Publications, Delhi-110 094, Lasertypeset by Gaurav Graphics, New Delhi and Printed at Himanshu Printers, Delhi.

Dedicated To

My Beloved Parents

Preface

Water is precious, and it is the free gift of the nature. Pure water is drawn from Lakes, Ponds, rivers, and perennial rivers. Water management and the distribution of water among the states are the most typical tasks. One of the salient features of our country is such that the availability of ground water is largely found in riverbeds, but the indiscriminate attitude towards the tapping of ground water is the sole reason for eco-imbalancing. Many MNC's and other popular branded beverages exploited it in fast manner and it would leads to the unnecessary problems. In future if World War-III may arises it is only due to the water problem. Under the reels of the liberalization, there is an urgent need for preserving this "Natural Gift" in a prolonged, sustained manner, not only for the present consumption, alone but also for future purpose. Since the commercialization of water in the global level also created an untoward incidents in many countries. This book made an attempt to manage the groundwater not only an efficient manner, but also in a very scarce manner.

I sincerely thank God Almighty for his blessings in completing my Project work successfully.

With immense pleasure, I express my heartful thanks to my guide and mentor Dr. R. Veerasekarn M.A., M.Phil., Ph.D., B.L.I.S., formerly state N.S.S. Liaison officer and Reader, Department of Economics, Urumu Dhanalakshmi College, Trichy-19, for his inspiring guidance, invaluable suggestions constructive discussion and encouragement during this project work.

I am equally thankful to my beloved brother, Mr. S.Chinnaiah, M.A., B.L., Inspector of Police, Prohibition and Enforcement wing Jayankondam, for his timely help and financial support.

My special and heartfelt gratitude's are due to My Beloved Wife. P. Kavitha, M.S., M.Phil., P.G.D.C.A., Lecturer in Physics Indra Ganesan Engineering College, Trichy and My Son Master A. Arun for their encouragement.

Next I leave it to the readers,

Suggestions for improvement are welcome.

Dr. S. ASAITHAMBI

Contents

1

Irrigation Institutions in a Dynamic Economy

Background

As water development concerns increasingly make way for water resource management strategies, discussions on water institutions in India and her south Asian neighbours are focusing on three key issues: *(a)* how to improve the performance and financial viability of public irrigation systems; *(b)* how to make groundwater use sustainable in economic and environmental terms; and *(c)* how to make a systematic transition from the water resource development mode to an Integrated Water Resources Management (IWRM) mode.

India is struggling on all three fronts. Its public irrigation systems are falling far short of their design potential for performance; they do not receive the investment they need for maintenance and upkeep; but above all, they are increasingly becoming a drag on state exchequer. Indian discussion on public irrigation systems is enamored by participatory irrigation management (PIM) and irrigation management transfer (IMT) as an 'institutional fix' for all these problems. However, despite two decades of experimentation, available evidence provides no indication that PIM works or will solve the problems public irrigation systems face. Similarly, India is stymied by its unregulated groundwater economy that functions as a colossal anarchy. Technocrats advocate strong regulatory frameworks; western experts argue for hi-tech approaches tested in the western US and Australia's Murray-Darling. In reality, policy action is paralysed by a political economy in which half of the country's population depends for livelihood on groundwater draft that is rapidly becoming unsustainable. Worse, thanks to perverse subsidies under its flat system of electricity pricing, India's booming groundwater irrigation economy has wrecked its energy economy.

The key challenges to rationalizing electricity pricing and supply to pumps are the huge transaction costs of collecting charges based on metered use and the fact that so many livelihoods have come to depend upon tube well irrigation [Shah, Scott, Kishore and Sharma 2004]. Much the same reasons defy the transition to IWRM: how to price water to reflect its scarcity value when water is such a volatile political issue? How to make an effective regulatory framework stick? How to unify fragmented water institutions? [Shah, Makin and Sakthivadivel 2001].

While India can provide its own answers to these questions, experiences from elsewhere may help guide its choices. However, as suggested above, looking to countries with far different social realities may not be the most helpful approach. Instead, examining the experience of nations which share at least some of India's fundamental conditions may be the more fruitful. Of those conditions, the most important may be *(1)* developing country status, *(2)* having a perceived need for water sector reform, and *(3)* large numbers of diffuse water users. India's neighbour to the north, China, has all three conditions. To gain an understanding of how the Chinese water experience might provide lessons for India, we combined literature review with two field visits in the Chinese provinces of Hebei, Henan, Shaanxi, Liaoning and Jiangsu during 2002 and 2003 which included visits to around 25 villages and discussions with officials of some 20 water bureaus at township, country, prefecture and provincial levels. The paper outlines a variety of ways in which China has acted differently from India, indeed all of south Asia, even as it struggles with the same set of issues those countries like India face. South Asian discussion and action on irrigation management reforms, groundwater management and IWRM seems stuck. The idea behind this paper is not to make a virtue out of the different route that China is following but to stimulate some out of box' thinking within India on possible ways out of its water woes.

Bounded Service Provider's as Managers in Small Irrigation Projects

One issue that most developing countries have not resolved satisfactorily is the management of irrigation systems, small and large. For long, governments have maintained large irrigation bureaucracies. However, bureaucratic management has been seen as a resounding failure almost everywhere; moreover, resource–strapped governments increasingly find irrigation bureaucracies a huge financial burden they are impatient to shed. During 1980s and 1990s, the idea gained ground that instead of through remote bureaucracies, irrigation schemes are best managed by organized and empowered farmer communities (Vermillion 1996 and 1999). As a result, PIM and irrigation management transfer IMT emerged as the 'ideal' institutional model. And many eager governments jumped on this new bandwagon with alacrity, especially when offered a cheap loan from an international donor.

However, after over 20 years of experience with IMT and PIM, old questions still remain unanswered. Does farmer management ensure better quality of irrigation service to farmers? Does it mean lower cost of O and M? does it result in improved productivity of irrigation water at the system as well as farm level? And better spatial and inter-personal equity in the allocation of water? Does PIM result in greater investment in maintenance and repair? And ease the financial burden on the state? To none of these has PIM or IMT offered an enduring answer. In the Philippines, initial years of the National Irrigation Authority (NIA)'s pioneering effort threw up positive results; but the performance of PIM has now slipped (Panella 1999). Where farmer management has improved cost recovery, it has done so by shrinking the command area served. In many Africa countries, PIM has done better where command areas populated by white commercial farmers with large holdings; but has left black smallholder communities worse off (Shah, van Koppen, Merry, Lange, Samad 2002). In Sri Lanka and Nepal, there are some success stories; but these need constant propping up. The latest experiment of large-scale PIM in Andhra Pradesh in India, which has been projected globally as a model, has already run out of steam even as several other Indian states have copied Andhra Pradesh's PIM Act (Reddy 1999).

One would have expected that after decades of Maoist experiments with variations of collective management in rural economy, Communist in China would take to ideas of community irrigation management with passion and zest. And everywhere we went, we found remnants of collective management. However, except where World Bank loans support PIM projects, China has not fallen for the communitarian model of irrigation organization. Instead, one witnessed everywhere variants of a model best described as 'bounded service provider', a private economic agent incentivised to perform a role assigned to him/her within a boundary established and defended by the village committee; hence our use of the phrase 'bounded service provider'.

This model is found most commonly with irrigation tube wells. Before the sweeping agrarian reforms initiated by the Deng administration after 1978, collectives throughout China were responsible for making and maintaining tube wells as well as pumps and distributions systems. With the onset of the household responsibility system (now defunct) and later reforms, a variety of institutional arrangements have now come into play in the Chinese countryside. Where water tables are high and tube wells and their operation inexpensive—as in parts of Henan province —village committees still own and maintain bore holes; but farmers bring their own or shared pumps; and the irrigation organization is quite akin to what we find in a south Asian village.

In deep tube well areas of Hebei, Shannxi and Shandong provinces, village irrigation organization undergoes marked change. Shallow and middle deep tube wells dominate the groundwater irrigation here as well. But we also find areas here with deep tube wells serving larger commands of 600-1,000 mu (approximately 40-70ha), whose construction costs are beyond the reach of most individual farmers. In these areas, it is still common for deep tube wells to be established, funded, and owned by the village development committee often by using accumulated savings, borrowing or imposing a new tax on farm land. Increasingly, however, village committees invite private investments, usually from farmers, to establish and operate tube wells as irrigation entrepreneurs (Lohmar et al 2002).

Thus the emerging Chinese management model for small holder irrigation systems is strikingly different from what we find in south Asia. Earlier, in the Maoist era, irrigation tube wells were directly managed by the village collective through salaried operators, much like public tube wells are still managed by government corporations in many Indian states. However, increasingly, O and M of these is commonly contracted out to a 'service providing entrepreneur' on a kind of franchise model. A variety of contracting arrangements seem to be in vogue; but variations were observed in five areas: *(a)* identification of 'service providers', *(b)* management fee; *(c)* responsibility of the contractor; *(d)* role of the village committee; and *(e)* impact.

Typically, 'service providers' are found from the more entrepreneurial amongst the village's farmers, men or women, only in one of the villages we visited did the irrigation system manager come from outside the village. In a few villages, a five-year 'management contract' was auctioned to the highest bidder. But a common procedure to identify and appoint the 'service provider' was informal negotiation by the village committee (VC) and/or the township water bureau (TWB) with prospective candidates. In some Shaanxi villages, where the TWB had built costly drip or sprinkler irrigation systems, we found the village leaders themselves, all men, had secured management contract. We also came across women managers of tube wells, one of whom took on the task not because it was remunerative but rather because she had been pressured by VC relatives to ensure continued operation. Where the management contract was auctioned, the village committees levied an annual fee on the contractors; however, this did not appear to be common and in these cases, the village committee still assumed the responsibility for maintenance and repair, and the manager was responsible only for water distribution and fee collection.

The period of the management contract varies from five to 30 years. The contractor's responsibility typically includes: *(a)* operation and maintenance of the system; *(b)* orderly distribution of water to farmers; *(c)* collection of irrigation fees; and *(d)* the payment of electricity fees to the village electrician or township electricity bureau. However, the irrigation fee is invariably determined by the village committee and/or the township water bureau; and this feature makes this arrangement different from outright privatization. There were too many variations in the way VCs determined irrigation fees to permit generalization; but fees are fixed in terms of hours of pumping or kWh of electricity uses[2]. In new drip or sprinkler irrigations systems in

Shannx, irrigation fees appeared high and the management contract lucrative. However, in some villages, we also found that pressure from farmers forced the VCs to keep irrigation fees low; and at least in one village, we found the contractor had terminated his contract and the village committee found a new contractor who also found that pressure from farmers forced the VCs to keep irrigation fees low; and at least in one village, we found the contractor had terminated his contract and the village committee found a new contractor who also happened to be the village electrician.

Our surmise is that the lucrative ness of the irrigation in franchise varied with contractor's contribution to the capital cost. In systems built, owned and operated by private farmers, the VC had little or no say in determining the irrigation fee. In some of the new drip and sprinkler systems, where contractors shared the capital costs, the VC had the power to fix the irrigation fee, but it allowed liberal margins and gave long-term contracts. We came across two such situations in Shaanxi; in one, the contractor shared less than 10 per cent of the capital cost and received a five-year contract; but in the other, the contractor contributed 25 per cent of the capital cost of a sprinkler irrigation system for which he obtained a 30-year management contract. Management contracts seemed to be the least lucrative on schemes wholly built and owned by VCs.

Entrepreneurial Managers in Large Irrigation Systems

When it comes to large irrigation systems, the picture is somewhat different and more diffuse. There are World Bank assisted PIM programmes like we have in Andhra Pradesh; but little is know about how well these have done. Jiangsu has one such project to organize water user association (WUAs); however, discussions with the provincial water bureau officials suggested that the project has not brought about much change. A key problem Jiangsu wanted addressed by PIM was the control of excessive use (around 15,000m^3/ha for rice) by farmers of expensive Yangtze water transferred from the south of the province to north. In the Jiangsu PIM project, the Bank funds were used to install meters at each WUA so that farmers could save in water fees if they reduced water use. Maintaining the meter, distributing water and collecting the water fee and turning it over to the local water bureau was all that the WUA did. The maintenance of canals and other infrastructure is still the responsibility of the local government.

Elsewhere, canal O and M, water distribution, and water fee collection in large irrigation systems are increasingly being taken away from village committees (or collectives), which had dominated irrigation management. This role is increasingly contracted out by the village leadership to private franchisees or WUAs of varied hue, often with strong financial incentives to save water and promote its efficient use. In a study of 51 villages from four irrigation districts in Ningxia and Henan, Wang et al (2002) found that between 1995 and 2001, the proportion of villages where collective management of irrigation systems fell from 100 to 27 per cent; that amongst the village that moved away form collective management, contracting to individual managers was twice as popular as forming WUAs; and that many WUAs were effective guise for management by the village leader himself.

Canal irrigation fees in many Chinese systems are levied in two parts: a basic water fee based on area irrigated and a volumetric water fee based on volume of water use. A part of the basic water fee collected is the contractor's fixed reward. However, the volumetric water fee based on area irrigated and a volumetric water fee based on volume of water use. A part of the basic water fee collected is the contractor's fixed reward. However, the volumetric water fee offers the contractor opportunity to increase his income by saving water. Before each cropping season, Irrigation district officials determine a target water entitlement for each village based on historical use patterns and other criteria, and value this entitlement on a volumetric fee. The total cost is apportioned to the farmland in the village, as an enhanced basic water fee from the farmers. However, he is required to pay to the water bureau only the volumetric rate on actual water use. By saving water, thus the contractor can enhance his earnings. The Wang et al paper (2003) showed that in the incentivised villages, water managers behaved significantly differently from the rest of the villages. In general they found that: *(a)* in villages with collectively managed systems, water use/ha was higher; *(b)* water use/ha was 40 per cent lower in villages with incentivised management; *(c)* shift to private contractor reduces water use/ha but more so when the contractor is incentivised; *(d)* water-saving by incentivised managers reduces water use/ha but more so when the contractor is incentivised; *(e)* water-saving by incentivised managers reduces wheat yields by 10 per cent, but maize and rice yields were not affected in any significant manner; and *(f)* in any case, these farmers either sustained their income levels or improved them despite low yields.

The China study by Wang et al, also found that while management reforms had gathered pace in Ningxia, they stagenatd in Henan. Their explanation was the drive for reform at the provincial level: in Ningxia, the Provincial Water Bureau pushed contracting energetically; in Henan, no such initiative was forth coming. A study of reform of public tube well management in Gujarat, India by Mukherji and Kishore (2003) concluded similarly: here too, management reforms succeeded because they were energetically supported and pushed by the top-levels of the irrigation department. Moreover, there is indicative evidence that incentivised irrigation managers have begun to worry about farmers turning to groundwater irrigation in the face of poor quality of surface irrigation service. In a Henan, Lohmar et al (2002) noted: "In these villages, it is interesting to see how the increasing use of groundwater has led to competition in the delivery of the village's water, forcing the surface system to improve its water delivery services".

All in all the direction in which institutional reforms in irrigation management are heading in China is different from south Asia where reforms are still shrouded in obscure communitarian logic. In PIM/IMT projects in India, focus of government, NGOs and donors is on organizing the communities, forming WUAs, capacity building, empowerment, and creating the right 'process'. There is little engagement with the nuts-and-bolts issues of managerial rewards and incentives, clarifying roles and responsibilities and, above all, getting results in terms of improved services, better fee collection, and more crop per drop. By focusing on creating 'bounded service providers',

China's re-forms seem focused on results. Nowhere in the course of out filed visits did we hear farmers or officials waxing eloquent about empowerment and capacity building. Instead, the institutional design discussion was centrally about shaping incentives, authority, checks and balances, and contract design and enforcement. Thus, the features of the 'Bounded Water Service Provider model we frequently encounter for small, self-contained irrigation schemes in rural China are best described as follows: *(a)* by insisting that the manager makes a substantial cash investment, it is ensured that he brings a serious intent or running a profitable water business for a long haul; *(b)* the seemingly high gross margin allowed makes it worthwhile for him to do proper O and; *(c)* wince the VC/TWB have some role to play in the issue water withdrawal permits by the county water bureau, they can, to some extent, ensure the manager's monopoly; *(d)* but at the same time, by insisting that the manager cannot raise the water price without the approval of the TWB, there is a built-in check on the exercise of monopoly power; and *(e)* since the village community has often no other alternative, a well-run, even if somewhat expensive, irrigation system would lift the entire economy to a higher plain of welfare.

Energy-Irrigation Nexus

A major cause of widespread groundwater depletion in India is perverse incentives created by energy subsides [Shah, Scott, Kishore and Sharma incur does not rise directly with growing scarcity of groundwater because of perverse energy subsidies. For instance, the cost of cubic meter of groundwater purchased by a small farmer is around Rs. 4-5 in eastern Uttar Pradesh or north Bihar in India where it is abundantly available but, it is less than Rs 2 in north Gujarat where it is mined from 800 feet or more. In Bangladesh, where ground, is abundant and can be pumped from 10 feet below ground, irrigating a hectare of paddy with purchased groundwater costs a high Taka 6,000 (Approx Rs. 4,800; US $ 100) [Mainuddin 2002, pers comm.] which drives many smallholders to manual irrigation; in contrast, in groundwater-stressed Tamil Nadu, where most groundwater presently begin used is mined, irrigating a hectare of paddy with purchased groundwater costs less than Rs. 1,500 because of electricity subsidies. This is not the case in China; as figure shows for nine villages of Henan and Hebei provinces we surveyed in 2002, irrigation cost as proportion of gross value of output rises in tandem with the depth from which groundwater is pumped.

The root of the problems is argued to be the transaction costs involved in collecting electricity charges from millions of farmers scattered over a huge countryside. The logistical difficulty and economic costs of metering electricity used by tube wells has been found so high that most Indian states have done away with metering and instead charge a flat tariff based on horsepower rating of the pumps [Shah 1993; Kishore, Sharma and Scott 2002]. Pakistan too tried flat tariff for nearly a decade before reverting to metering in 2000. In India, there is growing opposition to flat tariff in part because it is believed to induce inefficient use of power and groundwater but in part also because flat tariff has been used by populist politicians to subsides tube well irrigation. Electricity subsidy is thought to be the prime reason why many state electricity boards in India are on the verge of bankruptcy. Despite this state of affairs, some observers still argue that reintroduction of metering may not be a practical idea in the Indian context unless innovative technologies and/or institutional arrangements for collecting electricity charges can be used to reduces the transaction costs of metering and charge collection [Shah, Scott, Kishore and Sharma 2004; Godbole 2002]. All in all groundwater as well as power sectors in India are stuck in an invidious energy—irrigation nexus that does not augur well for either.

Surprisingly, the electricity-irrigation nexus is not a subject of discussion in China at all. The Chinese electricity supply industry operates on two principles *(a)* of total cost-recovery in generation, transmission and distribution at each level with some minor cross-subsidization across user groups and areas; and *(b)* each user pays in proportion to his metered use. Unlike in much of south Asia, rural electricity throughout China was charged at a higher rate than urban; and agriculture paid more than domestic and industrial use unit a few years ago [Wang et al 2004]. Unit 1997, the responsibility for O and M of the village electricity infrastructure and user charge recovery lay with the village committee. The standard arrangement in use was for the village committee and the township electricity bureau to appoint and train one or more local farmers as part time village electrician with dual responsibility, of maintaining the power supply infrastructure in the village as well as collecting user charges for a transformer assigned to him/her based on metered individual consumption from all categories of users. The sum of power use recorded in the meters attached to all irrigation pumps has to tally with the power supply recorded at the transformer for any given period. The electrician is required to pay the township electricity bureau for power use recorded at the transformer level.

This arrangement did not always work easily. Where power supply infrastructure was old and worn out, line losses below the transformer made this difficult. To allow for normal line losses, 10 per cent allowance is given by the township electricity bureau to the electrician. However, even this must have made it difficult for the latter to tally the tow; as a result, an Electricity Network Reform Programme was undertaken by the national government to modernize and rehabilitate rural power infrastructure where this was done, line losses fell sharply and among the villages we visited, none had a problem tallying power consumption recorded at the transformer level with the sum of consumption recorded by individual users, especially with the line-loss allowance of 10 per cent.

It is interesting that the village electrician in Henan and Hebei is able to deliver on fairly modest reward of Y200-250/month plus incentive bonus of around Y200/month [Zhang 2004] which is equivalent to the value of wheat produced on 1 mu (or one-fifteenth of the value of output on a hectare of land). For this rather modes wage, China's village electrician undertakes to make good to the township electricity station full amount on line and commercial losses in excess of 10 per cent of the power consumption recorded on the transformers; if he can manage to keep losses to less than 10 per cent, he can keep 40 per cent of the value of power saved. This generates powerful incentive for him to reduce line losses. In the way the Chinese collect metered electricity charges, it is well nigh impossible to make financial losses since these are firmly passed on downstream from one level to the next. Take for example, the malpractice common in south Asia of end-users tampering with meters or bribing the mater-reader to under-report actual consumption. In the Chinese system, it is very unlikely that such mal-practices can occur on a large scale since the village electrician is faced with serious personal loss if he fails to collect from the farmers electricity charges for al least 90 per cent of power for consumed as reported at the transformer meter. And since malpractice by a farmer directly hits other farmers in the village, there likely exist some peer control over such practices. In making metered power pricing work, China's unique advantage is its strong village level authority structure. The village committee, and especially, the village party leader, are respected and feared. These ensure that the electrician is able to do her job. In comparison to China's village committees, India's village panchayats are utterly devoid of power as well as authority as institutions for local governance.

In India, similar experiment is being tried out in Orissa where private companies in charge of distribution first experimented with Village Vidyut Sangha's (Electricity Cooperatives) but are now veering around to private entrepreneurs as electricity retailers. However, we do not have evidence on how well this arrangement is working. Even as India is taking small steps in the direction of private electricity retailing China is turning full circle. In its third phase of modernizing the electricity sector, electricity plants, transmission and distribution infrastructure are all now turned over to country electricity bureaus which have the responsibility of O and M of the infrastructure, of electricity delivery to households and other users, and of collecting user charges. Thus China is moving to a system similar to India's where state electricity boards (SEBs) directly serve hundreds of thousands of customers and collect user charges through their own field force. Expectedly, China will begin to face much the same problems in user fee recovery that Indian SEBs are trying hard to wriggle out of.

In many Chinese provinces, County Electricity Companies are therefore trying new ways of reducing transaction costs of collecting user fees for rural customers, especially irrigators. One of these is promoting pre-paid electricity cards or the IC car technology. The IC card system combines computer management, interactive card and single-chip auto control technologies. Its key benefit is that users need to pay electricity fee in advance to get their cards 'recharged'; moreover, IC cards can also be used for auto-irrigation and to record irrigation time. When the money stored in the card, is used up irrigation time. When the money stored in the card is used up, irrigation pump is switched off automatically. In recent years, the IC card system for the irrigation tube wells has been introduced in many water short provinces, such as Shandong, Hebei, Jilin, Heilongjiang, Liaoning, Inner Mongolai, Henan, Shaanxi, Jiangsu and Gansu.

A study commissioned by the IWMI-Tata programme to understand how the IC card system is working in Liaoning found that the main driver of the technology is the difficulty that township electricity companies and/or village committees faced in collecting electricity dues from farmers [Wang et al 2004]. The study also found that Chinese farmers are as resistant to the IC card system as south Asian farmers are to metering; and this resistance is not reduced the fact that the County Electricity Companies and Village Committees invest Y 800/tube well plus Y2000/ village on a computer/reading machine. Farmer resistance is understandable. According to Wang et al (2003), agricultural electricity bureau of Xinchengzi Region in Liaoning province could not collect electricity fees of about 2 to 4 million yuan/year from farmers have lost this hidden subsidy.

The IC card system keeps the county electricity company happy, because it eliminates all hidden subsidy. It keeps village committees happy because they are spared the hassle of collecting user fee from reluctant farmers. We would however expect farmers to be unhappy because of the new discipline to which they have to submit under the IC card system; but the Wang et al (2004) study concludes the majority of farmers interviewed to be happy because IC card system is 'fair', it reduces inter-farmer conflict on irrigation, and above all it drastically reduces the use of electricity and water, and thereby origination cost. As one farmer mentioned, "I save water, because now I see how much it costs".

Direct Regulation and Water Demand Management

Throughout south Asia, like in the north China plains (NCP), pockets where groundwater draft is exceeding long-term recharge are increasing by the day. Indian response to the challenge of sustainable groundwater management is however still muted. Political leaders still view groundwater professionals realize the need for applying brakes in growing pockets of resource over-exploitation and keep exhorting the need for strong legislation and regulatory frameworks. Many policy researchers, including the IWMI-Tata researchers, however, believe the case for direct regulation hopeless in south Asian settings, not because it is unnecessary or undesirable but on the grounds of administrative water withdrawal should be well nigh impossible to enforce on 20 odd million pump owners, a number that is growing at a rate of 0.8-1 million/year [Shah 2003], scattered across a vast countryside. The Indian experience with direct regulation so far has justified this pessimism [Shah 2004; Moench, Burke and Moench 2002; Phansalkar 2002].

However, under comparable conditions, China's experiences with direct management, even if not entirely positive, has at least shown some positive signs. Different provinces in the NCP have tried different combinations of instruments for direct demand management including: *(a)* tube well permits; *(b)* withdrawal permits; *(c)* differential and penal pricing; (d) direct regulation and sealing of wells; *(e)* creating alternative water supply; and *(f)* promotion of water saving technologies. The experience has been mixed; in general, these strategies have worked better on industries than on farmers, and in richer eastern provinces than in poorer western ones.

Table 1: Issues in Agricultural Water–Energy Nexus: China Versus India

	China	*India*
Energy fees proportional to use	Yes	No
Cost recovery in energy provision	Yes	No
Operator incentive for water efficiency and fee collection	Yes	No
Strong energy management oversight from village authorities	Yes	No

Water-energy nexus in considered an unresolved issue	No	Yes

Tube well permits do not control total groundwater draft but do act as a check on tube well numbers especially in over-exploited areas. Withdrawal permits are the most important direct management intervention and entail the registration of each user, allocation of quota to him/her, levy of a water resource fee, and the monitoring actual use vis-à-vis allocation much like a system that Mexico is experimenting without much success [Shah, Scott, and Buecheler 2004]. Water bureaus in some groundwater stressed regions at different administrative levels began experimenting with withdrawal permits as far back as in 1970s but without broader legislative support. However, real impetus came only with a 1993 regulation on Implementation Method of Water Withdrawal Permit System', under which any organization or individual who draws water from a river, lake or groundwater over certain levels must apply for a water withdrawal permit from the water resource bureaus (WRBs) at various government levels. The legal and policy support gained further strength more recently with the Water Law of 2002 which requires that old as well as new tube wells get withdrawal permits by July 1995. According to many observers, this is unlikely to be true even in 2002. In our discussion with Xingtai Water Bureau officials, of the 80,000 tube wells in use in the Hebei prefecture, only 30,000 permits had been issued so far. The same was the case in Liaoning, Henan, Shaanxi and Jiangsu.

Another problem in the utility of withdrawal permits is the collection of withdrawal fees from farmers. In the 1993 Regulation farmers were specifically exempted from the fee for a period of five years by the central government to alleviate their burden; and the exemption continues to date. Every once in a while, one comes across an interesting experiment at regulation such as the use of IC cards installed on each tube well such that it automatically shuts off once its allocated quota is pumped out, as we saw in Shaanxi. However, the general picture is that tube well as well as withdrawal permits have not brought any significant regulation of groundwater demand for irrigation. Wang and Huang (2002) suggested that water bureaus in Hebei were to begin collecting water fees from farmers irrigating with groundwater in 2000; however, in course of our fieldwork in Hebei in mid-2002 and again in 2003, we found no sign of farmers paying any water withdrawal fee in Hebei. Moreover, since most tube wells are owned and operated by village committees, permits are issued to them at a rate of 1 per village rather than per tube well. Similar was our experience in Liaoning which instituted Withdrawal Permits way back in 1978 and imposed a Water Resource Fee in 1987. Both these were enforced on industrial users and water companies even before the 1988 National Water Law gave a legal basis in support of such regulation; however, it is yet to touch agricultural use of groundwater.

Shaanxi has passed a slew of new water regulations in a quick succession: Water Pollution Control Regulation (1998); Flooding Control Regulation (1999); River Canal Management Regulation (2000); Urban Water Source Protection Regulation (2001); Water Saving Management Regulation (2003). These regulations are acquiring teeth because more and more water use is getting mediated; and institutions-water companies, irrigation districts, VCs–respond to regulations more quickly and readily than individual users. Through out north China, then, direct regulation is pursued vigorously with those segments of users who are easy to identify and regulate. For example, of the total of 23,800 permits issued by water bureaus in Shannxi, over 10,000 are to industrial users, irrigation districts and water supply companies supplying domestic and industrial customers. Where irrigation tube wells are operated by VCs, tube well permits are issued to them; but where they are individually owned, the picture is hazy and uncertain. With the segment of large users in the formal 'organised' sector, water budgeting too is done on an annual basis with a further set of deterrents as in the province of Jiangsu. Here, at the start of each year, water indents are called for from bulk water users by the provincial water bureau. The total demand is compared with supply and quotas are assigned. These are monitored at the end of the year; and users exceeding the quotas are penalized with a lower quota in subsequent year. Like Jiangsu, Shaanxi too distinguishers between water resource fee and water service fee but at woefully low rates of Y0.03.06/m^3 for surface water, Y0.08/m3 for groundwater and Y0.02/m^3 for spring water used by industry. Only industry is subjected to a water resource fee. Come 2005 and, we were told by WRB officials, the fee is being raised 10 times.

The experience of Shaanxi as well as Liaoning and Jiangsu suggests that the emergence of mediating agencies and bulk users makes direct regulation easier; it is easier to enforce withdrawal permits and levy resource fee on 'managed water' than self-produced water; and that pricing also works more easily with institutional users and 'managed' water. In Liaoning, for example, levying differential water resource fees for groundwater at Y0.55/m^3 in saline intrusion areas as compared to 0.3 Y/m^3 in normal regions has begun to reduce groundwater extraction in saline intrusion areas. Some industries have improved water use efficiency; others have closed down. And the bureau has used resources generated to bring surface water to increase groundwater recharge in coastal aquifers with some success.

Indirect Approaches to Demand Management

Groundwater demand for irrigation in some parts of rural north China is facing downward pressure because of unrelated wider trends which have no bearing on programmes and strategies evolved by water administration. A major factor has been the global decline in rice prices, which in recent years have drastically reduced profitability of rice cultivation. In Liaoning province, as a result, farmers have begun shifting wholesale form irrigated rice to rain fed maize. Especially in rice areas, falling rice price have combined with rising costs of energy in pumping groundwater from deep tube wells to form a pincer that is driving tube well irrigated rice out of the market. According to Lianoning Provincial Water Bureau officials we met, this pincer-besides controls in industrial use of groundwater-has helped raise average depth to the water tale from 34m to 18m in the province.

This became clear to us in our visit to Youtai village, near the city of Shenyang in Lianoning. This village like others in the region has only 1 crop of rain fed maize in a year, planted in may and harvested in October. After that the climate is too cold for farming.

Rain fed maize and irrigated rice are the alternative from which farmers choose. And rain fed maize is becoming increasingly popular. Maize yields at 800kg/ mu are higher than irrigated rice at 600kg/mu. The prevailing farm gate price of both are similar at Y 1.1 kg. But rice is far more input intensive-especially in fertilizer, water and labour. Wage rates are Y30/day. A hectare (=5 mu) of rice requires 400-500 hours of pump irrigation. As a result, input costs of irrigated rice may be as high as Y 500-600/mu. Not surprising that of the 5,096 mu of farm land in this village, only 1,000 mu are under rice; 3 years ago, the proportions were the opposite of this.

In Hebei, Bt cotton is increasingly replacing maize-wheat combination that has prevailed during recent years in many areas; and the Chinese government is proactively encouraging this shift, only partly because Bt cotton uses far less water compared to the maize-wheat combination. That has prevailed during recent years in many areas; and the Chinese government is proactively encouraging this shift, only partly because Bt cotton uses far less water compared to the maize-wheat combination. For one, land plated with Bt cotton remains fallow the rest of the year in many areas. Then, Bt cotton needs only one, at most tow irrigation; whereas wheat needs at least 4-6 irrigations although maize is mostly rain fed. Above all, cotton is not only amenable to drip irrigation but has a strong positive yield response. As a result, we found large areas of Bt cotton farmers in Hebei and Shandong taking to drip irrigation to save pumping costs and raise crop yield. There is also massive adoption of plastic mulch as a device to reduce evaporation of water and moisture preservation in Hebei and

Shandong provinces. Farmers we met claimed large electricity cost savings and significant yield gains. That there are significant yield gains from mulching seems also indicated by the fact that farmers spend & 25-30/mu to lay mulch, and that local shops stock polythene mulching material is indication that demand is mainstreamed. Near Feixiang on the border of Shandong province, we found extensive use of plastic mulching in even rain fed Bt Cotton. The women farmer we interviewed plated Bt cotton only if there is rain. But for the past 2-3 years, she has begun using plastic mulch at a cost of Y 20-25/mu, which helps to greatly improve the root zone moisture regime and improve crop yields.

Bt cotton seems extremely profitable with gross income at Y 1,300-1,500/mu and input costs at Y 300/mu. This makes it attractive to farmers. And because it saves groundwater, intervening around it has become popular with VCs and WRBs in groundwater stressed areas. In Dagao village in Nangong county (Xingtai prefecture, Hebei), the key problem is salinity in shallow aquifers and water tables falling @ 1 m/year. Several micro-irrigation projects are established here. In one such that we visited, of the 3,500 mu or irrigated area, 1,000 were under Bt cotton, and over 50 per cent of Bt cotton mu were under drip irrigation installed by the VC from its won funds. Some 80 old shallow tube wells (5KV), privately owned, are now in use only for supplementary irrigation. In 1995, 9 new Deep TWS (30 KV) were installed by the VC at a cost of Y 1,20,000 Y 70,000 for Deep TWs and Y 50,000 for buried pipes) each commanding 300mu. Farmers asserted great advantage of drip irrigation. Earlier, irrigation all the 500 mu took the VC 1 month; now it is done in 1 week. Water use has fallen from 50m3.mu to Y 7/mu. And cotton yield has increased, according to farmers interviewed, from 150kg/mu to 225kg/mu. Enthused by the results, the VC is planning to cover all 3,500 mu under drip irrigation, which essentially is 'drip irrigation' since no micro-tubes are used. Before the drip system was installed, it took 1.5 hours to irrigate a distant mu; now, 1 hour's pumping irrigates 4mu.

Table 2 : Water Pricing in Jiangsu

User Category	*Water Resource Fee (Y/m^3)*	*Water Supply Cost (Y/m^3)*
Groundwater Pumpers	2	0
Domestic customers	0.03	0.04
Industrial	0.03	Supply cost=2-10% margin
Irrigation	0	Y 5-12/mu for rice Y 0.6-3/mu wheat

Promoting the shift from wheat-maize combine to Bt cotton, promoting drip irrigation and mulching in Bt cotton aided by high and rising costs of electricity—all these are emerging as indirect instruments of controlling groundwater demand in north China plains.

Arresting Urban Groundwater Depletion

Like elsewhere in Asia, Chinese cities are facing unprecedented groundwater stress. The strategy many Chinese provinces find effective to control urban groundwater depletion is three-pronged: *(a)* import surface water from distant sources and use it to crowd out urban tube wells; *(b)* as alternate sources become available seal urban tube wells in a campaign mode; and *(c)* begin to enforce withdrawal permits strictly once alterative water becomes available; and *(d)* use a penal water resource fee on groundwater to reflect the scarcity value of groundwater and promote substitution of surface water for groundwater.

Much evidence in Chinese cities suggests that depletion of urban aquifers is best countered not by demand management, which certainly plays a role, but by crowding out urban tube wells through water imports. Shaanxi as well as Jiangsu offers good examples of how such a strategy works. Until 1990, urban tube examples of how such a strategy works. Until 1990, urban tube wells supplied 8,00,000m^3.day to urban population resulting in serious depletion of Shaanxi's urban aquifers. Now, surface water imports supply 1.2million m^3/day. All urban tube wells are closed and, according the officials of Shananxi Water Resource Bureau, water tables are now rising @ 1-1.5m/year. All new urban water supply projects are based on surface water imports. Xian, the capital city, gets its water from a reservoir 40km away.

Jiangsu, next only to Shanghai and Guangdong in industrial progress and per caput income, has experienced intensive groundwater use in the industrial and domestic sectors in large part because its use carried no or very low fees. As a result, in many urban areas, groundwater tables had fallen to 40 m or more; and tube wells were typically 80 or more meters deep. To ease the pressure on groundwater, the province implemented a south-to-north water transfer project of its won within the province using lifted Yangtze water. This water is priced according to a different formula; since the water has to be lifted to a considerable height at five different places, there is a significant fixed as well as variable water supply cost. To reflect this, the water price too has a flat (basic price) and variable component (volumetric, based on metered use).

Having created a new supply source, the province began enforcing water permits and put into place t two-part pricing formula providing for a water resource fee and a water supply fee (Table 2). In this new formula, groundwater is priced way above even lifted Yangze water at Y 2/m^3; as a result, industries as well as water companies have begun substituting surface water for groundwater. All (non-irrigation) is issued a withdrawal permit, accompanied by a card which records the complete tube well profile as well as pattern of pumping and use of groundwater. A total of 4,830 tube wells have been so covered by the formal regulatory system in three cities of the province. Along side, the WRB has also launched an intensive water saving programme; some 1,000 industries are involved in experimenting innovative water saving technologies.

As a result of this extensive direct regulation, since 1995, the province has made a big impact on reducing urban groundwater depletion. From 2001, Jiangsu Provincial WRB has begun a campaign to close urban and industrial tube wells; 3,100 tube wells have already been closed; and the WRB target is to close all tube wells by 2005. Not surprising then that groundwater depletion has not only been arrested but water tables in many urban areas have begun rising by up to 6 m/year. Jiangsu's experience suggests that where alternatives are available and dependence on groundwater is low, proactive demand management not only becomes feasible but quite easy.

Size and Penetration of Water Bureaucracy

One reason why China has aggressively pursued direct management in water resources sector is its huge, 6-layered water bureaucracy presided at the top by the ministry of water resources. The real operating agencies are however parts of the hierarchy of water bureaus at provincial, prefecture, county and township levels which generally constitute the operational arms of water administration within the various provinces. India is notorious for its bloated bureaucracy; but the Chinese employ far more bureaucrats in managing water resources. Hebei is a case in point. Xingtai prefecture, one of Hebei's 11, along has a total of 20,000 employees in water resource bureaus and other water organizations in the prefecture. In Liaoning province, some 40,000 government staff are employed in water bureaus at different levels, excluding an equal number at village level. Gujarat is bigger than Liaoning, but has just around 11,000 public officials employed by water related departments; most of these are engineers hired for construction of projects; very few public officials are devoted directly to water resources and service management at the district level and below; and this size too is shrinking.

In China, water bureaus are substantial outfits even at the county level (equivalent to 2-3 taluks /blocks/ tehsils in south Asia). In Ci county in Hebei province, which has 19 townships and 390 villages under it, the county water bureau staff is only 60 and a typical township water bureau employs 20-30 officials; however the entire hierarchy of water bureaus in Ci County employs some 560 people. Hebei province, for instance, has mine city level water bureaus and 200 water bureaus of counties like Ci, which manage water resources in 4,000 small townships and village. Thus, when all levels are taken together, the water bureau structure in a province may employ several tens of thousand officials; and these do not include village and some of the township level water officials who are paid wholly from local taxes and water fees. Whereas the provincial water bureau is fully supported by the state budget, the county water bureau has to raise a portion of its won budget and the township water bureau and village water administration is wholly self-financed. Thus, Ci county in Hebei has an annual budget of & 30 million; of this, in 2002, Y 10 million was contributed by the national government under drought mitigation programme but the balance of Y 20 million had to be raised from farmers' taxes and local incomes. Kendy et al (202) note, in their study of groundwater institutions and polices in Luancheng county near Beijing that fee revenues are sufficient to fund the County Water Affairs Bureau, but not to fiancé water conservation countywide".

Having a large bureaucracy with deep penetration and presence at local and meso levels has its pros as well as cons. The Chinese bureaucracy has been a subject of much criticism. However, the powerful role it can play in the governance of scarce natural resources such as water is often underestimated. In India, the Supreme Court announced too far-reaching environmental decisions during the past decade: first, it enjoined the forest department to halt illegal felling of trees in reserved forest areas forthwith; and the forest department effectively implemented the Supreme Court's injunction throughout Indian countryside because it has a large field force with significant presence at the local levels. In 1996 the same Supreme

Court designated the Central Groundwater Board of India as the nation's Groundwater Authority and mandated it to control groundwater over-draft forthwith. Six years later, the Central groundwater Authority has remained totally ineffective to implement the Supreme Court mandate mainly because it has no field force worth the name.

India has got so disillusioned with its bureaucracy that all its energy is focused on shrinking it rather than vitalizing it. Irrigation departments of most Indian states have recruited professional engineers only for constructing irrigation systems; now that the construction phase is over, these have failed to transform their professional workforce for resource management and service provision roles. As a result, irrigation bureaucracy is increasingly begin viewed as a drag on the public exchequer; and many states have not recruited professional staff in irrigation departments for the past 12-15 years; and according to one analysis, Gujarat's irrigation department will shrink from a total strength of 11,000 engineers to less than 500 be 2010 because those who superannuate are not replaced. At the Same time, we find that the government's presence in water management role at district, taluka and village level is either very thin or absent. China's focus on transforming bureaucrats into entrepreneurs is of relevance to India because the role of the state will have to grow—not shrink—as the stress on water resources grows further. For, leave alone direct regulation, even indirect instruments of water management require a bureaucracy to implement.

Institutional Reform

Compared to south Asia's fragmented water administrations, China's water affairs bureaus represent an effective first step towards integrating and unifying water management tasks at local levels. Until a decade ago, water management in a typical county in China was fragmented as in a south Asian local administrative territory (such as a tehsil or a district). Before then, water supply and sanitation and infrastructure construction was managed by the urban construction bureau; water companies were controlled by urban management department. Groundwater was under the ministry of geology and mines. And water saving technologies was the responsibility of the ministry of agriculture while power plants and electricity transmission and distribution infrastructure in many provinces were owned and managed by water bureaus.

A serious—and avoidable—water crisis in Shenzhen in 1991 led its municipal administration to create a water affairs bureau which integrated all tasks and functions concerned with water source development and construction, flood control and drainage infrastructure, urban water supply and sanitation, water affairs bureau model caught on like wildfire; and by May 1999,160 countries had reorganized water resource bureaus into water affairs bureaus. In May 2000, Shanghai brought in even more functions under a new Shanghai Water Affairs Bureau [Wang and Huang 2002]. From the groundwater perspective, another major 1998 reform was to remove groundwater management from the ministry of geology and mines to the ministry of water resources, a more logical home.

We heard the echo of this bottom-up institutional reform backed by top-level legislative action (2002 Water Law) wherever we went. In Shaanxi, converting erstwhile water resource bureaus into water affairs bureaus has been done in a campaign mode. Until recently, urban water supply was managed by urban construction bureaus. Now there is a growing movement to shift this to water affairs bureau. Of the 100 County WRBs. In Liaoning, too, 11 counties and four cities have already converted to water affairs bureaus since 1997. All 11 counties in Xingtai prefecture in Hebei province have converted into water affairs bureaus, which manage water companies; only Xingtai City's water supply is managed by a company owned by urban construction bureau.

In Jangsu, we found transition to the water affairs bureau structure was progressing at different pace in different parts of the province. Suzhou city, for instance, has a WAB that integrates all key water management roles: water supply, issue and enforcement of withdrawal permits, collecting pollution fees, water resource fees, all under one roof. Elsewhere in the province, the restructuring is still in progress. Despite this uneven pace of reform, Chinese researchers believe that unified water resources management under the overall leadership of the much-restructured MOWR is gradually becoming a reality in China [Wang and Huang 2002].

Increasingly, water affairs bureaus are strongly encouraged to adopt a business rather than regulatory-bureaucratic approach and generate resources locally by selling services. True, this may be easier said than done, especially since revenue yielding water infrastructural assets are often still held by provincial bureaus or the national government. Hebei, for example, has tow large reservoirs which might yield substantial income from water sale to industries and municipalities; however, these are under the direct control of the national government. In Ci County Water Bureau in Hebei, the new drive towards local resource generation is already beginning to change the culture of the bureau. The River Basin Management office made & 2 million last year by selling irrigation to farmers @ Y 10./1000m^3 of Zhuang River water to irrigate 60,000 mu. Ci county water affairs bureau also has a separate company to manage urban and industrial water supply from groundwater. Industries either get water from the company or obtain a licence and make their own tube wells by paying the water resource fee. These are closely monitored and closed if the resource position is inadequate.

Conclusion

Hence, we have suggested that China is refreshingly unorthodox in exploring unique solutions to its context, which, in several respects, is more similar to south Asia's than of the industrialized west where south Asia tends to look for solutions. It is by no means our contention that approaches China is trying are necessarily appropriate for other countries or even that they will solve China's problems. We are also not suggesting that China's performance on Integrated Water Resources Management is about to meet international standards. In fact, a UN Expert Committee studying Huiahe basin wrote in 2000 that, "Water use and abuse in the Huaihe basin is effectively anarchic with very limited enforcement and compliance" [UN 2000]. However we do suggest that south Asian discussions on water reforms need to incorporate a wider body of experience; as such, Chinese explorations appear one appropriate candidate. From examining the Chinese experience, three sets of conclusions can be drawn with direct relevance to south Asia.

First China has already given up on traditional communitarian model of organization of managing its small-scale groundwater based irrigation system as well as large irrigation projects. Instead of participatory management by water users' associations—except on World Bank funded PIM projects—China has experimented with a variety of models of irrigation service providers' who are incentivised for better service delivery improved water use efficiency and better performance in water fee collection. It is not clear yet how well this arrangement is performing; in the case of small-scale systems, indications are that incentivised service providers promote efficient water use, besides improving fee collection.

Second, north China's agrarian economy is as precariously dependent upon high-energy use in pumping groundwater as south Asia's is. However, the huge transaction costs of metering a large number of scattered tube wells has forced south Asia to adopt flat electricity pricing which is more prone to subsidization, while China, in a similar situation, has struggled to make metered electricity supply and full cost recovery work in agricultural power supply. This has not been easy; but significant gains seem to have been achieved by incentivising village electricians to operate as commission agents of the township electricity bureau. More recently, many Chinese provinces have been experimenting with EC pre-paid electricity cards for agricultural electricity supply. Many Indian states—

where subsidised flat electricity tariff is wrecking groundwater as well as power industries—are struggling to reintroduce metering. China's experience can provide useful guidance in this direction.

Third, north China has made quite some progress in getting some modicum of control over runaway groundwater over draft by using a combination of direct as well as indirect instruments of demand management such as promotion of water saving approaches and technologies, implementation of withdrawal permits pricing of water resource as well as services, enforcement of water withdrawal quotas, crowding out urban tube wells by surface water imports and such like. Doubtless, these measures have been more effective in urban areas than in agriculture, and in economically more dynamic eastern provinces compared to agricultural western provinces. However, after years of regulatory activism there is growing confidence amongst Chinese water professionals that they can achieve their own version of IWRM which, at the ground level, means *(a)* bringing all water management roles under water resource bureau structures; *(b)* broadening water resource bureau roles by rechristening them as water affairs bureaus; *(c)* instituting a system of water withdrawal permits; *(d)* imposing and levying a water resource fee in addition to water service charges; *(e)* countering urban groundwater depletion through import of surface water from distant projects; and *(f)* by reorienting its massive eater bureaucracy from water development to resource management mode rather than by shrinking it.

2

Trends of Ground Water Irrigation in India

This section is based on a large resurvey of villages, after a gap of 20 years, in the eastern and western regions of Uttar Pradesh. Some of the findings from the study indicate that significant changes have taken place during these years in the two regions in respect of socio-economic features, role of groundwater irrigation including groundwater markets, productivity of crops and changing face of the rural elite. The most important trend is that the high-caste supremacy in terms of ownership of modern agricultural implements is on the wane, while backward castes are surging ahead in such ownership.

Niranjan Pant

The section is based on a larger study [Pant, 2003] conducted in four districts of Uttar Pradesh. Of these, two each were in the western and eastern regions. Further, in two of the same villages were surveyed where the author had done a study in 1981-82. Thus, villages from Meerut (west) and Deoria (east) were those studied earlier, while new study villages were selected in Moradabad (west) and Jaunpur (east) districts. The selection of village studied earlier was done with a view to compare the past and present findings. In all, 12 villages were selected, of which four were studied earlier, and eight were few. Of the latter, four each were from Moradabad and Jaunpur.

Although the eastern and western regions of Uttar Pradesh both from part of the Gangetic plain, the two present a picture of contrast. The eastern tract is flood-prone with periodic occurrences of droughts and is less developed. It is characterized by impeded drainage leading to water logging during the rainy season, affecting sowing and crop yields. The western tract, although receives much less rainfall, is assisted by old canal networks and high development of groundwater resources.

In an effort to determine the extent of disparity between the two regions, we have detailed the key indicators of development in Table1. Theses indicators have been clubbed under four headings dealing with: *(a)* general features *(b)* infrastructure facilities *(c)* credit facilities, and *(d)* agricultural development. It is obvious from the data that, eastern region lags behind the western region in all the positive indicators of development, but is ahead in indicators that show to backwardness. It comes out as a socially and economically backward area with large concentrations of poor farmers and a preponderance of small and marginal holdings. Foods afflict a large part of the area. In the absence of adequate credit facilities, the resource base of farmers is meager; as result, a small area is covered by commercial crops. This is further aggravated by lower cropping intensity and low crop yields, which ultimately leads to reduction of gross value of agricultural produce.

Socio-Economic Features

Table 2 captures important economic aspects of the two regions. The 1981 survey data has also been included in the table to enable comparison in respect of Meerut and Deoria [Pant 1984]. The first point to be noted is that the average landholding size has shrunk in both regions during the past 20years. In the two villages of Meerut, the average land owned per household has come down from 5.7 acres to 3.7 and 3.9 acres. In Deoria, land owned per household has fallen in Pakri Babu, but in Kusmauni the land size has increased. The main reason for this is a significant proportion of the village households (in our sample 20 per cent) are employed in North-Eastern Railway and that these households have purchased land in the Village. As a result, the average size has gone up in the sample.

However, the significant fact to be noted is that in all villages except Nagli Issue in Meerut, the average number of parcels per hectare of land has come down significantly and the average size of parcels has increased. Overall, the average land owned has declined from 2.6 acres to 2 acres in the east and from 4.84 to 2.46 in the west. As far as reduction in landholding size is concerned, it is mainly influenced by population pressure. In fact, per capital availability of land has declined over the years. In UP the per capita reporting area was 0.29 ha in 1971; this declined to 0.27 ha in 1981 and 0.21 ha in 1991.

The one positive aspect the comparison between the two surveys is the household size and literacy. While household size has marginally reduced in all the villages, the literacy rate has made a quantum jump, from 37 per cent to 68 per cent in western UP and from 40 per cent to 64 per cent in the eastern part.

An important component of agriculture is the participation of male and female members. Comparison with past data reveals that participation of males as well as females has increased in agricultural operations during the past 20 years in all the villages. About 48 per cent males were engaged in agriculture in 1981 their proportion going up to 79 per cent in 2002 in the east, while in the west their proportion increased from 47 per cent to 86 per cent. In case of female members in the east, 22 per cent participated in cultivation earlier but now 45 per cent participate. In the west, female participation has gone up from 21 per cent to 35 per cent.

The table also contains data in respect of leasing in and leasing out, which is legally not permissible, and a landholder is supposed to carry out cultivation himself [Sonkar 1989: 8-9] except under certain circumstances. Despite the legal restriction, leasing activities go no routinely. However, respondents try to conceal facts relating to leasing. Therefore, during the survey it was very difficult to get the actual position in respect of leasing. Generally those leasing in are more open about it than those who report leasing out. This can be seen if we compare the figures of those who lease in and lease out. It would be seen that the percentage of households who lease in is generally much higher than those who lease out. This phenomenon has been found in other studies also, such as Dubash (2002:55), MDP (1997: 74-75) and Pant (1992: 22-24). This trend is also a natural outcome of the fact that generally fewer larger farmers lease out lands to numerous marginal or landless farmers.

If we compare the data of the 1981 and 2002 surveys, it is found that the proportion of those who lease in land has gone up in all the villages of Meerut and Deoria, and that land leasing is a widely prevalent reality in spite of the legal restriction. If we compare past and present data, it is found that as against about 12 per cent of the households who used to lease in land in the east, now 26 per cent of the households do so. The Change is more dramatic in case of the west, where earlier only about 3 per cent of the households leased in land but now about 18 per cent of the households do. Among the five villages where leasing is widely prevalent, Mohammadpur Emma is the only one where larger farmers lease in land from smaller ones. In the other four villages (all from the east), generally marginal farmers lease in land.

If the leasing activity is examined in relation to landholding size, significant differences are noticeable. In case of western UP, 50 per cent of farmers who lease in land are households with less than 1 acre holding, 30 per cent own 1-2 acres of land and 20 per cent own more than 2 acres. In contrast, in the eastern region farmers with less than 1 acre land dominate the leasing in (80.6 per cent), while landowners having more than 1 acre account for just 20 per cent of all leasers. In respect of leasing out, the reporting is mostly from the western region. Here, the overall picture shows that 72 per cent of those who lease out own more than 2 acres of land the 14 per cent each belong to the land ownership categories of 1-2 acres and less than 1 acre. In the category of less than 1 acre it was found that leasing in and leasing out was going on hand-in-hand and in realistic terms it was more of an informal exchange of parcels of land.

In comparative terms, while in the west leasing in is common among all categories of farmers, in the east it is largely a marginal farmer syndrome. In fact, Kripa Shankar, who did a field survey in Junpur in 1979-80, found an almost similar trend where most of the leasing in was done by marginal and small farmers, while leasing out was more visible in larger holdings. The most noticeable fact, however, was that the category of 2.5 and 5- acre landowners constituted the dominant actors in leasing in as well as in leasing out [Shankar 1986: 7-12]. Our findings are similar.

Table 1: Indicators of Development in the Eastern and Western Alluviums of UP

	Particulars	*Western*	*Eastern*	*UP*
1	General			
1.1	Population in million (1991)	49.5	52.7	139.1
1.2	Geographical area in sq km (1991)	82191	85844	2944111
1.3	Density of population per km (1991)	603	614	473
1.4	Per cent of urban population to total UP SC population (1991)	26.3	11.6	19.8
1.5	Per cent of literacy (1991)	42.0	38.5	41.6
1.6	Per cent of scheduled castes in total UP SC population (1991)	31.5	37.3	100
1.6a	Per cent of SCs in each region to total regional population (1991)	18.6	20.7	21
1.7	Average monsoon rainfall in mm (2002)	765.7	891.3	NA
2	Infrastructure			
2.1	Per capital electricity consumption (kwh 1998-99)	206.8	169.2	184.9

2.2	Per cent of electrified village (March 31, 2000)	88.8	77.0	79.0
2.3	Post office per lakh population (1998-2000)	9.8	13.1	13.9
2.4	Telegraph office per lakh population (1998-99)	0.4	0.8	0.8
2.5	Telephones per lakh population (1999-2000)	1520	778	1246
2.6	Length of metalled road under PWD per 1,000 sq km (1999-2000)	422.2	409.8	369.9
3	Credit Facilities			
3.1	Credit deposit ratio (June 1999-2000)	22.5	22.0	21.6
3.2	Scheduled commercial banks per lakh population (1999-2000)	5.2	5.3	5.3
3.3	Co-operative agricultural marketing centres per lakh population (99-2000)	3.1	1.8	2.2
3.4	Co-operative marketing societies per lakh pop (1999-2000)	0.17	0.11	0.16
3.5	Joint agricultural co-operative societies (1999-2000)	1.0	0.6	0.8
4	Agriculture Related			
4.1	Per cent of marginal holdings (<1 ha, 1995-96)	66.8	83.0	75.4
4.1a	Per cent of area under marginal holdings (1995-1996)	28.1	44.8	33.7
4.2	Average size of marginal holding (ha 1995-1996)	0.42	0.35	0.39
4.2a	Per cent of small holdings (1-2 ha) (1995-1996)	17.8	10.9	14.6
4.2b	Per cent of area under small holdings (1995-1966)	24.9	22.8	23.8
4.2c	Average size of small holdings (1995-1996)	1.42	1.36	1.41
4.3	Per cent of farmers against main workers (1990-91)	47.9	54.8	53.3
4.4	Per cent of agricultural laborers against main workers (90-91)	18.5	22.5	18.9
4.5	Consumption of electricity in Ag As per cent of total con, 1998-99)	43.4	25.0	31.0
4.6	Cultivable area as per cent of reported area (1994-95)	82.7	77.0	70.9
4.7	Net cultivated area as per cent of cultivable area (1998-99)	90.8	86.1	83.4

4.8	Net irrigated area as per cent of net cropped area (1998-99)	89.7	61.4	72.2
4.8a	GIA as per cent GCA 1998-99	83.9	60.4	67.6
4.9	Per cent of area irrigated by state tubewells (98-99)	3.8	10.1	5.8
4.10	Per cent of area irrigated by private tubewells (98-99)	75.6	59.5	63.5
4.11	Per cent of balance GW to total safe yield March 31,2000	34.0	54.0	46.0
4.12	Cropping intensity (1998-99)	156.0	150.8	148.8
4.13	Commercial crop area as per cent of gross cropped area (98-99)	32.1	10.4	20.5
4.14	Per cent of kharif area affected by floods (1999-2000)	0.92	8.5	3.9
4.15	Availability of tractor per gross cropped area (in ha 98-99)	32.1	74.4	47.1
4.16	Distribution of fertilizer per ha on current prices (97-98)	148.1	116.2	118.2
4.17	Value of Agricultural Produce per ha on current prices (97-98)	21280	15677	17857
4.18	Productivity of food grains (q/ha 98-99)	24.1	19.2	19.4
4.19	Productivity of wheat (q/ha 98-99)	303.3	22.2	25.2
4.20	Productivity of rice (q/ha 98-99)	22.0	18.4	19.4
4.21	Productivity of potatoes (q/ha 98-99)	250.3	200.5	228.2
4.22	Productivity of Oil seeds (q/ha 98-99)	8.9	5.5	7.0
4.23	Productivity of sugarcane (q/ha 98-99)	621.9	466.0	589.9
4.24	Gross value of Agricultural Produce per rural person on current prices (97-98)	3447	2435	3594
4.25	Income from primary sector as per cent of net domestic output (97-98)	38.6	36.3	36.9

Note: UP incudes Uttaranchal which is a separate State now.

Source: District wise Indictors of Development -2000, Economics and Statistic division, State planning institute, GoUP, 2002

Crop Productivity

The first noticeable thing in Table 3 (based on the 2002 survey) is that although productivity of crops is generally higher in the western districts, in case of mustard, pulses and coarse grains productivity is higher in the eastern region. Secondly, even in base of sugar cane, paddy and wheat, where yields are higher on the western region, the gap is not very wide. Thirdly, there is no systematic region wise demarcation in the levels of productivity. There are some villages where yields are good, while there are others where yields are not so good or are even poor irrespective of whether such villages form a part of the eastern or eastern region. Chakra, and to some extent Kurni in Janupur show very good yields the other shows better results in respect of sugar came. Fourthly, the yields coming out of our survey are generally higher than those reported in official statistics (Table 1). Yields presented in Table 3 are comparatively much higher in case of paddy, wheat, oilseeds and potato than reported in Table 1 and except in case of sugar cane.

The yields have witnessed a tremendous upward swing compared with those what was noted during out 1981 survey. At the time the average yields were 20.5 qtl/ha for wheat, 21.7 qtl/ha for paddy and 426.5 qtl/ha for sugar cane [Pant 1984: 182-83]. In another survey which was done in 1990 in the eastern region in the districts of Faizabad and Bahraich), the average productivity of paddy was found to be 38.2 and 34.6 qtl/ha (Faizabad/Bahraich), while that of wheat was 31.2 and 28.5 qtl/ha in Faizabad and Bahraich respectively [Plant 1992:90]. If we compare these figures with those of the present survey, paddy shows a decrease in productivity while wheat shows some increase in eastern UP. Here it would be useful to note that there are variations in productivity levels within eastern UP also with some areas where productivity is as good as in Haryana and Punjab and others where productivity is very poor. In fact, it is not unusual to find villages in eastern UP where

Table 2: Main Socio–Economic Characteristics of Sample Households (1981 Included)

(Land in acres)

	District / Village & year of Survey	Average hh Size	Literacy (%)	Participation in Agriculture (%) M	F	Total	Average Land Owned Per hh	Average No of Parcels Per hh	Average Size of Parcel	% of hh leasing in	Average Area Leased in Per hh	% leasing Out
	Meerut											
1	Nagli Issa (2002)	7.3	80.0	87.2	50.0	69.3	3.69	3.56	1.04	10.0	0.75	-
1a	-do- (1981)	7.5	35.7	43.0	23.3	34.7	5.70	3.96	1.44	6.7	2.97	-
2	Modkalan (2002)	6.6	65.0	92.7	53.8	63.8	3.85	2.81	1.37	5.0	4.0	-
2a	-do- (1981)	7.7	38.1	51.0	19.1	37.2	5.70	5.72	1.00	-	-	-
	Moradabad											
3	Mundha Pande (2002)	9.5	70.0	80.0	3.4	43.5	3.78	2.15	1.76	20.0	0.54	10.0
4	Dalpatpur (2002)	11.2	65.0	73.0	33.3	53.7	2.52	2.30	1.09	15.8	1.67	5.0
5	Mohd Pur Emma (2002)	8.2	70.0	88.7	32.6	65.7	3.73	2.30	1.62	45.0	1.48	15.0
6	Singhpur Saini (2002)	8.1	60.0	93.2	51.2	76.0	2.90	1.80	1.61	15.	0.53	-

	Jaunpur											
7	Chakra (2002)	8.2	60.0	70.9	17.9	44.1	3.01	2.28	1.32	30.0	0.59	5.0
8	Deolaspur (2002)	10.2	55.0	82.4	69.6	76.1	1.88	2.10	0.90	5.0	1.00	-
9	Purwa (2002)	10.4	45.0	70.8	67.3	69.2	1.56	1.55	1.00	30.0	1.05	-
10	Kurni (2002)	6.7	70.0	85.4	59.5	72.3	1.30	1.90	0.68	45.0	0.76	-
	Deoria											
11	Kusmauni (2002)	8.4	70.0	84.3	30.8	61.1	1.86	1.65	1.13	10.0	0.50	-
11a	-do- (1981)	8.1	32.0	47.5	12.2	30.8	1.50	2.09	0.72	-	-	1.0
12	Pakri Babu (2002)	9.0	85.0	80.3	21.2	53.1	2.41	1.65	1.46	35.0	0.75	-
12a	-do- (1981)	9.1	49.5	48.1	18.8	35.4	3.60	3.13	1.15	25.0	0.89	6.52
	Western UP (2002)	8.4	68.3	85.5	34.7	60.9	3.41	2.46	1.39	18.49	1.32	5.0
	-do- (1981)	7.6	36.9	47.0	21.2	36.0	4.70	4.84	0.97	3.33	2.97	-
	Eastern UP (2002)	8.8	64.2	78.5	44.7	62.4	2.00	1.85	1.08	25.83	0.77	0.83
	-do- (1981)	8.6	40.2	47.8	21.5	33.1	2.60	2.61	1.00	11.98	0.89	3.64

paddy yields are as high as 51 qtl/ha and that of wheat 41 qtl/ha [Hallabh et al 2003]. Even among the households surveyed by us in 2002, of the ones whose crop productivities were the highest, the largest proportions were drawn from Chakra and Kurni Villages of Janupur district in eastern UP and not from Moradabad or Meerut in western UP.

Two things that made all the difference in productivity were the soil type and quality of land and the availability of reliable sources of irrigation water. In two of our previous studies this aspect was examined. In our 1984 study, we found that the highest wheat yields of paddy were those who got canal water adequately. In case of sugar cane, the highest yields were obtained by those who combined anal water with their own groundwater resources in the form of tube wells/pumpsets [Plant 1984: 182-183]. The 1992 study was confined to groundwater resources consisting of public tube wells funded by the World Bank and private WEDs. In that study, for both Faizabad and Bahraich those who combined public tube well irrigation with their own WED obtained the highest yields of wheat and paddy. The lowest yields in case of wheat in both districts was obtain by those who bought groundwater from others. However, in case of paddy the lowest yields were obtained by those who irrigated their crop from public tube wells, while those who bought water obtained much better yields than many others [Pant 1992:90].

A common feature noticed during the 2002 survey was that all cultivators strived to attain the highest yields in all study villages. For similar land quality, farmers seemed to know the village-specific combination of inputs and generally used the same and obtained similar yields. This contention is also supported by another recent study [Ballabh et al 2003: 26]. Even resource-poor and marginal farmers were able to meet the productivity related requirement of crops such as HYV seeds, fertilizers, insecticides/pesticides and irrigation. A common feature noticeable in case of marginal farmers was that they resorted to non-farm income to generate money to meet crop requirements. So it was commonly observed that when a household needed crop inputs and the need for a particular input was critical, adult members of the household would go out of the village to work as daily wage workers to meet the requirement. Thus, non-farm income constituted an important part of the agrarian economy in both regions of UP.

Growth of Private Tube Wells and Diselisation

Sick public tube wells hit but power shortage, mechanical defects and declining discharge in water on the one hand [CAG 1982, Shankar 1982] and increasing demand for timely and adequate amounts of water due to introduction of HYV seeds and greater productivity of crops on the other, led to stupendous growth of private tube wells in UP from about 3,000 in 1951 to 6,00,000 in 1977 [Dhawan 1982] and to 1.05 million in 1980 (Table 4). By the mid–1970s, tube well irrigation had overtaken canal irrigation, which was the dominant mode or irrigation earlier. The rapid growth or private tube wells had it s repercussions on the power sector. Historically, as groundwater development was taking place in the state, the demand for power was not significant in rural areas and surplus power was available until the 1970s. However, by the early 1980s, large-scale groundwater development in the private sector had led to a situation where rural demand for electricity always exceeded availability. It was around this time that power generation and transmission capacity became the constraint to the rate at which electrical connection to tube wells could be made.

Table 4 shows data from 1980 onwards on various modes of groundwater extraction prevalent in the two regions of UP. Traditional modes of groundwater irrigation, that is dug-wells and Persian wheels, seemed to be quite popular in both regions until mid-1980s while Persian wheels continued to be popular. Between the two regions, dug-wheels to be more popular in the eastern region. Persian wheels seemed to be equally popular in the two regions although marginally more so in the western region.

In respect of diesel pump sets, it is found that there has been a progressive increase in their number in the tow regions. But the growth of diesel pump sets was more pronounced after the mid-1980s in the eastern region. In fact, after 1993, the growth of diesel pumping sets is higher in eastern UP in comparison with the western region. The reverse is noticed in case of electric tube wells. Here up to 1984-85, growth was faster in eastern UP, which growth was higher in western UP. In this respect, what is noteworthy is that, there is a decline in the growth of electric tube wells between the mid-1980s and mid 1990s in both regions and the decline is more severe in case of eastern region. However, there is a growth again after the mid–1990s and it is faster in the eastern region.

The proportion of diesel pumps in total pumpsets was also always higher in the western region. It increased from 59.3 per cent in 1980 to 64.5 per cent in 1985 and then to 78.6 per cent in 1994, after which it registered a marginal decline of 0.7 per cent. In the eastern region, the picture is quite different. Here, the proportion of eclectic pumps was more than diesel pumps in 1980s and 1985, at 58.7 per cent and 52.5 per cent respectively. A dramatic decline, however, occurred in the number of electric tube wells between mid-1980s and mid-1990s when the proportion of electric pumps declined to 13.4 per cent. During the same period, the proportion of diesel pumps recorded an overwhelming increase from 41.3 per cent to 86.6 per cent of the total pumpsets. After the mid-1990s, and till 1998-99, like the western region, the eastern region also recorded a marginal decline of 0.5 per cent in share of diesel pumpsets.

The inevitable conclusion the data provides is that the power position in eastern UP deteriorated rapidly between the mid-1980s and mid-1990s when many villagers discarded their electric tube wells. The author witnessed this phenomenon when he conducted tow surveys in eastern UP in 1989 and 1990. In fact during the first survey, the author had found the actual availability of electricity in the World Bank-funded tube wells to be 8.6 hours per day for Basti and 9.5 hours per day for Deoria. This was despite the fact that these tube wells were connected with a dedicated power supply which was to provide them an average guaranteed supply for 18 hours per day [Pant 1989]. In our 2002 survey we found that power supply was available for 6.2 hours per day in the villages of the eastern region and 6.3 hours per day in the western region.

One significant trend emerging from Table 4 is that

the power position has improved in both the regions during 1994-99 as indicated by a marginal increase in growth of electric tube wells. However, the validity of this trend appears questionable if we compare it with field-level data collected for the larger study, particularly in respect of the eastern region, which after 1991 has witnessed de-electrification.

Table 3: Productivity of Main Crops in Sample Villages

(Qtl/ha)

District / Village	*Sugar Cane*	*Paddy*	*Wheat*	*Mustard*	*Mixed (Wheat+ Mustard)*	*Pulses*	*Coarse Grain*	*Potato*
<u>Meerut</u>								
Nagli Issa	602.8	26.7	44.5	14.1	-	7.7	19.8	
Insignificant								
Modkalan	600.1	37.1	32.6	10.1	30.1/4.9	6.2	-	-
<u>Moradabad</u>								
Mundha Pande	585.5	34.3	36.1	8.2	30.8/6.2	8.2	-	-
Dalpatpur	-	37.1	37.6	9.4	-	8.4	-	-
Mohd Pur Emma	624.9	38.8	41.5	9.1	35.1/4.9	8.2	-	
Insignificant								
Singhpur Saini	646.2	42.3	45.5	9.4	-	7.2	-	
Insignificant								
<u>Janupur</u>								
Chakra	624.0	42.7	45.2	17.0	-	14.8	28.4	323.3
Deolaspur	524.9	31.4	29.2	14.3	29.2/4.2	12.1	17.5	250.0
Purwa	610.7	32.5	33.4	10.6	28.8/6.2	11.4	15.4	194.0
Kumi	667.7	35.1	34.6	14.8	-	13.1	19.0	226.4
<u>Deoria</u>								
Kusmauni	530.3	43.0	36.8	-	-	14.1	-	-
Pakri Babu	574.5	27.4	31.6	15.8	-	13.2	-	178.6
Western Region	612.2	38.3	38.8	10.1	31.4/5.3	7.2	19.2	-
Eastern Region	590.7	35.3	35.9	14.8	29.4/5.5	13.8	20.7	224.6

Note: All cultivators were not able to assess productivity. Hence productivity figures are based on the assessment of farmers who clearly explained their productivity (2002 Survey).

Free Boring Scheme

The origin of the free boring scheme can be traced to the RBI report of 1984 which recommended a heavy does of subsidy for the development of groundwater in eastern India. Following this report, the government of UP launched a targeted free boring scheme. Under the programme, free boring facility to the extent of Rs. 3,000 was provided to small and marginal farmers. Additionally, subsides of 33.3 per cent and 50 per cent were provided to small and marginal/SC and ST farmers respectively of PU used its own financial resources to enhance the rate of subside provided by the GoI from 25 per cent to 33.3 per cent and from 33.3 per cent to 50 per cent [Pant 1991].

Some researchers regard the free boring scheme, as it operates in the state today, as a model to be followed by other east Indian states, including West Bengal (reference). They might be correct in their assessment. The author's own position in this respect is that the whole programme was based on the easy availability of vast sums of money which were to be exhausted each year without any mid-course review and evaluation or does monitoring and physical verification of what was happening in the field. It is possible that the present set-up consisting of dealer-farmer relationship is the best course of action. Yet we have to establish the extent of its success through some kind of review based on field-level data. Unlike many other centrally sponsored rural development schemes, the free boring scheme was not subject to any such evaluations. The target achievements claimed in respect of SC/ST beneficiaries, particularly after the mid 1990s, appear quite unrealistic and exaggerated.

In addition, there are vast differences between the free boring figures supplied by the district and state-level authorities. Besides these unpleasant foot [Pant 2004]. In such a scenario, a quick study of the free boring scheme in all its ramifications in UP is an absolute must before the scheme is recommended as a model for the rest of eastern India. The study may also examine the worthiness of dealer-farmer relationships and suggest ways and means to reduced transaction cost without inflating suvidha shulk' to an unreasonable level so as to genuinely become a blueprint for the rest of eastern India. The need for such a study increase manifold in the light of our recommendation that more liberal subsidy needs to be given in eastern UP to check the menace of waterlogging, and enhance cropping intensity and crop production.

Groundwater Markets

Localised informal sale and purchase of groundwater extracted through pumpsets as an important source of irrigation must have been witnessed by many researches since the emergence of tube well technology in India. In fact, the author himself found this phenomenon during his survey of irrigation system in 1981 and had put this practice under the others sources category [Pant 1984a:172]. There were also others who had witnessed the strong presence of this phenomenon [Prasad et al 1984, Jairath 1985]. But it required the understanding, foresight and genius of Tushaar Shah, who by the mid-1980s had visualized transforming groundwater markets into powerful instruments of small farmer development" [Shah 1985]. Shah, with his continuing research—alone and in association with others [Shah and Raju 1987, Shah

1987]—had argued that although private exploitation of groundwater was by definition inequitable, it did leave the poor better off in an absolute sense that is, efficient water markets can maximize benefit of private exploitation of groundwater for poor sections of the community. By April 1989, when a World Bank symposium on groundwater and rural poor in south Asia took place in Washington DC, the idea and terminology propounded by Shah had acquired widespread use and acceptability. Shah further consolidated his findings in his later works to greater higher of theoretical propositions [Shah 1993, 1999, 1999a, 2001]. In fact, all the research on groundwater markets whether dealing with India, Nepal, Pakistan or Bangladesh is an appendage to Shah's works and ideas presented earlier in various papers, reports and seminars.

In the context of Uttar Pradesh, all the discussions regarding groundwater markets have focused on their role in eastern Up mainly because of the useful role groundwater markets play in tackling the issue of access to groundwater for the poor and remedying the problem arising due to lack of consolidation of holdings. Yet, as we have seen, groundwater markets have been equally important in the western region of UP also; at times it has been more significant in western UP than in the eastern region. This has clearly emerged from a recent study of groundwater markets in Meerut district [Singh and Singh 2003:118]. Groundwater markets have played a significant role region. Our research had so far indicated that groundwater markets solved the problem of scattered holdings in the eastern region [Pant 1992: 36-37]. This point has been substantiated by others [Ballabh et al 2003: 28]. It is true even in respect of western UP. In western UP the number of parcels of land have come down in recent years but even today their average number remains at 2.5 per hectare (as per out 2002 survey). In such a scenario, the groundwater market is a great contributor.

Judging groundwater markets from the angle of their accessibility to poor and marginal farmers, it is found that the smallest farmers with landholdings up to 0.4 ha are the biggest beneficiaries, as about 60 per cent of them irrigate their crops using water purchased form the owners of private WED. As against it only 7 per cent irrigate their crops with water from public tube wells [Pant 1992].

Finally there is overwhelming evidence that during the decade of the 1980s there was a coincidence of class and caste and ownership of water extraction devices as well as a positive relationship with the size of landholding. The data from the author's past surveys also confirms the class-caste coincidences as we find a positive relationship between high castes, ownership of modern agricultural implements and landholding size however, the trend cases to exits as we examine our 2002 survey data and take modern agricultural implements into consideration. The 2002 survey data seem to demolish the high-caste supremacy in terms of ownership of modern agricultural implements. Backward castes seem to surge ahead or go neck-and with high castes in owning such implements. Many factors are responsible of this change. One the back wad castes represented by Yadav, Kurmi, Koyeri in eastern UP and Jat and Gujjar in western UP represent a sturdy group of hard working cultivators who are the biggest beneficiaries of the zamindari

Table 4: Number of Groundwater Works in Eastern and Western Alluvium

No. of the End of Year	Dug-well			Persian Wheel			Diesel Pumping Set			Electric Tubewell		
	East	West	Up	East	West	Up	East	West	Up	East	West	Up
1979-80	271151	258583	679443	15338	179410	239671	128954	317028	581998	183083	217432	465969
	53.60	46.64	46.14	41.06	41.65	36.36	16.30	11.72	9.38	24.94	21.17	23.08
1984-85	228655	222371	586119	15500	179786	245022	258727	526343	1030488	285902	290068	674753
	45.20	40.11	39.80	41.11	41.74	37.18	12.61	19.46	16.61	38.95	28.24	33.43
1993-94	NA	NA	NA	NA	NA	NA	525389	710862	1624923	81431	194027	306978
							25.61	26.29	26.20	11.09	18.89	15.21
1998-99	6110	73430	207042	71540	71540	174371	1138065	1149837	2965357	183623	325743	270748
	11.20	13.25	14.06	16.61	16.61	26.46	55.48	42.52	47.81	25.02	31.71	28.28
Total	505916	554384	1472604	430736	430736	659064	2051135	2704070	6202766	734039	1027270	2018448
	100.00	100.00	100.00	100.00	100.00	100.00	100.00	100.00	100.00	100.00	100.00	100.00

abolition. In due course these castes with their numerical strength and sound agricultural base found adequate representation in political institutions representing power. Their hold got further consolidated with the implementation of Mandal Commission recommendations, when they began entering bureaucratic corridors of power. Therefore, it appears quite realistic that they pep resent the new rural elites. Similar trend of consolidation of backward castes in rural Bihar in the late 1970s was reported by the author in the context of block level officials and politician [Pant 1979: 29-31].

Apart from this main trend, the following other trends are most visible. First, public irrigation as a means of irrigation has diminished during the past 20 years. The deterioration is greater in the western region compared with the eastern region. Further, to be noted between the two public sources of irrigation, dependence on canals seems to be greater than on state- owned tube wells in the west, while dependence was greater on state tube wells in the east. However, public irrigation systems still remain important in combination with other sources such as own source or purchased water as about 27 per cent households in the east and 9 per cent households depended exclusively on their own sources 20 years ago, now none has such a privilege as they a have to depend on purchased water apart from their own source to meet their irrigation requirement. Third, and most important, is that an overwhelming proportion of households depend on groundwater markets for their cropping. Further, between diesel and electric pumpsets, while village wise differences remain, in overall terms, diesel pumpsets are a more common source of irrigation in both scenario can be gauged by the fact that in the west 40.8 per cent sample respondents depend on it now compared with 28.3 per cent 20 years ago. In the east, about 16 per cent depended hose who depend on it along with their own source or use of public source are in such a high proportion that it points on an inevitability of water markets in the present times on the Gangetic plains. Fourth, the present study has also dictated that consolidation of holdings completed in tow regions has proved to be beneficial to farming households. Although no clear-cut relationship can be established on the of the present study, it can be safely assumed that the agricultural growth in eastern UP has been greatly facilitated on account of successful of consolidation of holdings. Fifth, among all categories of farmers, generally those belonging to the landholding category of more than one acre and less than 2.5 acres of land were found to be the most active farm leaders in al agrarian enterprises and more often than not belonged to a backward caste.

3

Improved Water Control as Strategy for Enhancing Tribal Livelihoods

Synthesizing the lessons of a two-year collaborative research programme by researchers and NGOs, this section suggest that improved water control strategies, designed after taking contextual factors of resource conditions and socio-ecology into consideration, have a high potential of redressing the livelihood problems of India's most neglected people, besides also leading to sustained and salutary impacts on wider human development indicators for this region. While other development intervention are also important and necessary, public investment in assuring improved irrigation water control can act to kick-start the tribal economy in the region.

I. Genesis of and Motivation for Research

The central Indian tribal homeland, located between

18 and 25 degrees north of the equator across the India sub-continent, operationally cover nearly 100 districts in eight states of the country stretching from Banswara (Rajasthan) in the west to Purulia (West Bengal) in the east (Figure 1). These districts together account of about 55 million tribal people (roughly 70 per cent of India's tribal population) spread over 68 million hectares of geographic area and having access to about 45 million hectares of cultivable land. The region is well endowed in terms of rainfall and vegetative cover and yet, is home to one of the largest concentration of rural poor in the world. Central India Initiative (CInI), a collaborative research programme between the international Water Management Institute (IWMI); Sir Ratan Tata Trust (SRTT), Mumbai; Professional Assistance for Development Action (PRADAN), New Delhi and the NM Sadguru Water and Development Foundation (NMWSDF), Dahod, is aimed at identifying factors that lead to successes or failures of water-centric live hood intervention among the tribal people in this region. The initiative recognized that improved water control strategies would not only help strengthen tribal livelihoods, but also transform the tribal homelands into future granaries for the country.

Three aspects make the research subject of CInI important: *(i)* if it is possible to implement appropriate water control strategies for enhancing tribal livelihoods on a large scale, it would lead to significantly enhanced incomes and employment in the tribal areas, resulting in much reduced hunger, food insecurity and forced migration of the tribal-people; *(ii)* these efforts would result in significant addition to national food production and contribute towards strengthening the food security of the nation in the long run; and *(iii)* these efforts would create incentives for the tribal people to work as a community in retarding and reversing the rapid degradation of the natural resources in their habitats. As a noted NGO leader points out unless quick action is taken, several hundred square kilometers of tribal homelands will become depopulate, leaving a vast degraded land mass behind. This paper synthesizes and summarizes the results of 40 odd studies undertaken in CInI on the theme.

OVERVIEW OF RESEARCH

Tribal Context

Tribal districts identified under CInI have lagged behind other areas of the country on several indicators of development. For instance, Phansikar (2003) has noted that these tribal districts form a majority of the 71 most underdeveloped districts of the country. Debroy and Bhandari (2003) have prepareda list of some 69 backward and most–backward districts of the county and as many as 30 districts identified for CInI find a place in their list, along with other districts of Uttaranchal, Uttar Pradesh, Bihar, West Bengal and the north-eastern states, many of which also have large tribal population. It presents some important parameters reflecting on the level of development in these districts vis-à-vis national averages.

Data from a primary survey of more than 800 tribal and nontribal farmers undertaken by CInI in seven tribal districts across seven states [Verma, Nair and Sharma 2004; Verma, Dasgupta and Singh 2004;] as well as data from 10 district studies undertaken as part of CInI reveals that: *(i)* tribal farmers derive much less income from their lands than their non-tribal brother even in the tribal-dominated blocks of tribal districts; *(ii)* their net returns from agriculture are also much lower; *(iii)* they make much smaller investments (in absolute rupee terms) in agricultural assets as compared to the non-tribal while the proportion of their capital investments devoted to agriculture is much higher indicating their desire and willingness to increase the productivity of their agriculture; *(iv)* they have much seeker access to agricultural technology and inputs form the state or private sector machine; and *(v)* the dependence of tribal propels on income from seasonal migration, often under surges, is twice as high as that for non-tribal people from the same districts.

What could be the possible explanation for these differences? There are some hints in existing literature. There is a fairly articulate view that seeks to project tribal communities as being distinct in their cultural ethos and life pattern form the rest of Indian society. This view holds that tribal people are the un-spoilt children of nature who seek to live in harmony with nature but suffer due to ossified production conditions [see, for instance, Sreeparampil 1996]. They do not have a sharply defined notion of private property and the resources around them are seen to be meant for the nurturance of every one. The forest provides for their simple needs and its this resource abundance and communal partaking form 'Mother Nature' that traditionally kept them away from the need and concepts of resource-use intensification and settled farming. Even though how the ground reality around the tribal communities has changed or is fast changing with rapid depletion of forests and dispersion of tribal people, they attempt to guard the essence of their way of life and are reluctant to resist or lack the necessary attributes for acquisition and for intensification of resource use.

Boserup (1965), in a similar vein, tries to explain this gap using the concepts of resource conditions and population pressure. She suggests that resource-use intensification occurs under pressure of population. Tribal people have traditionally lived under conditions of relative resource abundance (low population density: high rainfall and high vegetative cover) and hence were never compelled to intensify the use of their resources such as land (through increased cropping intensity) and water (through irrigation). Likewise, Pfeiffer (2003) talks about differences between immediate and delayed return systems to explain how the nature of resource-use would be different under the two system. There are other arguments that explain the low productivity of tribal agriculture as a result of systematic sate neglect. Finally there is a school which looks at tribal farmers as rational economic actors, not very different form other peasants (for example, see Paty 1992 and Mukherjee 1982 among others). The proponents of this view argue that tribal agriculture continues to suffer because: *(i)* tribal people do not have the security of tenure (they often live in reserve forest areas): *(ii)* the chance of meeting own consumption demand through alternate options such as migration is high; *(iii)* there is neither any security of savings nor any convenient investment option available; and *(iv)* cash is always at a huge premium and cost of capital prohibitively high for them. This view thus implies that security of tenure, comparative economics of options (comparison in terms of leisure income trade-off as well), and a facilitation of savings as well as investment will induce tribes to take to intensive agriculture like it does for every one else.

Implication from the Study of Interventions

Eighteen sets of interventions have been studied in CInI over two years. These interventions can broadly be divided into five groups: *(i)* supporting and building upon spontaneous community action based on traditional wisdom (as well as schemes that followed essentially the same logic); *(ii)* interventions that installed irrigation shames or enable tribal people in achieving greater water control; *(iii)* watershed development programmes being implemented in various parts of the central Indian tribal heartlands; *(iv)* impact of the inter-play of market forces on tribal farmers; and *(v)* comprehensive 'Water PLUS' intervention aimed at rehabilitating tribal people and sustaining their livelihoods on their respective resource bases. We briefly discuss inferences from each of these categories of studies.

The 'community action based on traditional wisdom interventions are those that have emerged as a response of the communities to changes in their specific resource conditions, essentially to protect their paddy crop from water stress induced by erratic monsoon. Dabaris (smaller versions of the famous Chandela and Malugzari tanks), for instance, were essentially created as storages of surplus precipitation. Several of them face the same fate as other tank systems elsewhere: ill-defined ownership and stake in the changing context; absence of well-defined governance norms to replace the erstwhile feudal norms; disrepair of dabaris and implemented a large programme for supporting and building new debaris all over the state. These interventions seem to be oriented towards subsistence rather than growth and the case studies provide little evidence that these structures led to creation of marketable surplus or the onset of a market oriented agriculture that creates capital for reinvestment. Therefore, while fit well with the local socio-ecology and need to be they involve troubling questions regarding their durability be context of unchecked onslaught in the tribal heartlands. Studies of state as well as civil society ed irrigation inter indicated that so long as the four steps, viz., proper me design, mobilization of the beneficiary groups, sound procedures, and provision of auxiliary inputs, are incorporated, large-scale group lift irrigation schemes replicable models of tribal livelihood enhancement. It be noted that all these schemes have demonstrated huge for enabling the tribal people to take much enhanced from their land. Several of them—notably the Sadguru irrigation (LI) schemes a majority of PRSFSNLI schemes AKRSP (India) supported participatory irrigation management PIM schemes have realized this potential to a commandant extent. However, there are various question which must swerved before such interventions are planned for large-scale mentation: *(i)* are the tribal communities ready for irrigated *(ii)* should one attend to social institutions first? *(iii)* Group schemes a must? *(iv)* Do they have to be managed people form the very start?

Table 1 : District level comparison of Tribal Districts in Central India with All-India Averages

Parameter	*Average for Central Indian tribal Districts*	*All-India Average*
How Tribal Districts are Better-off		
Population density*	200.23	324.00
Per cent of forest area*	32.75	19.39
Sex ratio*	970.00	927.00
Under 6 sex ratio*	954.00	933.00
Female work participation (per cent*)	26.92	23.26
How Tribal Districts are Worse-off		
Per cent of rural population**	85.35	74.29
Infant mortality rate*	81.78	72.77
Per cent of population below poverty line*	42.67	26.00
Extent of hunger (% households going hungry)*	5.63	2.96
Literacy*	60.09	65.38
Average CMIE's Index of development*	84.09	100.00
Irrigated are as per cent of cultivated area**	11.00	34.00
Fertiliser consumption (kg/Ha)**	32.32	63.88
Average value of14.98 crop output (Rs per Ha)**	2697.55	8578.00
Per cent of net irrigated area to net sown area**	14.98	33.59
% of net area irrigated by major irrigation systems**	3.66	9.89
Per cent of net area irrigated by minor irrigation**	16.83	42.28
Groundwater**	11.32	24.28
Surface lift irrigation**	5.51	18.00

Notes: * Average for districts in central India based on data from 70 most tribal districts

** Average for districts in central India based on data from 30 most tribal districts.

Sources: Shah and Singh (2003); Census of India (GoI 1991); Profiles of Districts- centre for Monitoring the Indian Economy [CMIE 1993; CMIE 2000] Debroy and Bhandari (2003).

Communities across these studies face differing resource and have had varying levels of exposure to settled-farming it would appear that the western Indian tribal communities acute resource pressure and have been fairly exposed communities and their agriculture practices. Post to this they have a clear and articulate demand for in the case of eastern Indian tribal communities the resource pressure is milder and their exposure to agriculture has been limited. Further, stream-based LI usually do not address the key issue of stabilizing kharif and create an unwarranted competition between rabi and migration based livelihoods.

Studies on watershed development programmes suggest livelihoods-centric and tribal-friendly approach to water the standard watershed projects follow a procedure and the dominant ideology is that of the who are interested more in soil and water (SWC) measures for long-term, survival of the in those resource setting puritanical watershed programmes discourage any water harvesting as the extraction of water more or less negates effects of conservation. Community interests, on the and often tend to be more immediate. We find that the earthwork involved in watershed development projects creates employment for two-three years for the poor. The lure of this wage employment close to their homes makes tribal communities excellent partners in the implementation of these projects. The activities such as Continuous Contour Trenching (CCT) and Water Absorption Trenching (WAT) undertaken on hill sides do improve the overall moisture regime and increase water levels in wells but the benefits accrue disproportionately in favour of the people living in the valley portion. However, when the standard, methods are modified to include activities of direct relevance to tribal people, the degree of benefits received by them can change drastically.

The studies on the impact of market forces on tribal

farmers raise the fundamental issue of designing technologies that are suitable for smallholders and at the same time ensuring prolific market development for these technologies so as to reach a large number of poor at affordable prices. The study of sprinklers in Narsinghpur, for instance, shows how a beneficial technology when marketed by profit-seeking players reaches the tribal people after a huge delay and even then serves only the creamy layer among them. While these methods do not create water resources, they lead of efficient use of available water. Therefore, the success of the private sector model of development, critically depends upon the ability to create and development critically depends upon the ability to create and develop markets for the product or services among the poor. They require the state or donors to invest in market creation which alone will led to large enough demand to make private sector participate even at low product prices. By the preference so far has been on upfront subsidies: Capital subsidies in conventional water resource development of direct product subsidies as in the case of drips and sprinklers which often fail to reach the poor.

Finally, the studies on Water PLUS; interventions look at attempts to rehabilitate tribal people through comprehensive land and water management interventions. The Bharatiya Agro Industry Foundation (BAIF) approach is to create microenvironments' in small plots of land using whatever sources of water that can be tapped. At core to the whole programme lies the concept of a wadio or a small plots by farmers and they are encouraged to take inter-crops of marketable vegetables and other cash crops so that they derive some income even during the long gestation period of the wadio. Besides the wadip programme, BAIF has also initiated several other programmes including those aimed at increasing agricultural productivity, drinking water provision and women empowerment. Another unique feature of BAIF's efforts is that they had built grass roots institutions which gradually take over the operations and management of their programmes and with time, their own role changes form being the implementing agency to that of one providing technical backstopping. BAIF has managed to lift over 18,000 tribal families out of the poverty trap through this approach and it has taken them over a decade to evolve the total package of practices.

The PRADAN case study [Chakraborty 2004] documents efforts taken to persuade farmers from the Santhal tribe to adopt modern farming technologies and practices with a view to stabilizing the kharif paddy crop. The intervention involves sample steps: better land preparation; carefully choosing high quality seeds and treating them before use; better nursery management; and better nutrient management. It demonstrates that tribal people are concerned with the extra expenses and risks associated with more input intensive agriculture in the context of uncertain water control. Wherever water control is achieved, technology adoption is much faster and the results are very satisfactory. Tribal farmers with no water control and poor upland plots have difficulties in taking to and benefiting from such techniques.

Crosscutting Issues

In this section, we review the work done of four crosscutting themes and aspects of water control as livelihoods enhancement strategies. The first pertains to availability of water on a sustained basis to implement water control based livelihoods strategies. This is relevant since tribal people live in upper reaches of river basins and at least theoretically, their use of water reduces its availability to communities living in middle and lower reaches of the same basin. The initiative undertook work no simulating the level of water-use development in a basin to assess the extent to which further development can take place without giving rise to situations of sharp conflict between upstream and downstream user [Verma, Ghosh and Seshadri 2004]. This basin simulation model grapples with the complex question of working out inter sub basin flows in the context of uncertain rainfall. Using data for a small basin in Dahod district of Gujarat and the conceptual framework developed by IWMI [Molden, Sakthivadivel and Samad 2001], it shows how the level of basin development can be estimated and how the time to reach full utilization can be computed under various assumptions and scenarios. Higher and more secure rainfall, low population pressure and low levels of basin developments perhaps permit much higher harvesting and use of water in the eastern basins. It suggests that undertaking such basin simulation may be useful in deciding the overall strategy for water control in a basin. Further, it indicates the need to explicitly factor—in the stage of development of a basin into the design of interventions, especially for the water-stressed and often over-appropriated western parts of the central Indian tribal homelands.

The second pertains to socio-technical aspects of water control strategies and the fit of types of technology with diverse conditions where a matrix of technologies in use across the central Indian tribal homelands has been studies [Satpathy and Naik 2004]. This study groups the intervention modes into hands-off and hands-on approaches. In the former, an intervener, usually an agency of the state creates or supports water control hardware and leaves it in the hands of the people without further engagement. This, for instance, happens when a medium or minor irrigation scheme is created, a large group lift irrigation scheme is installed or a combination of well and a pump is provided on subsidy to the people. The hands-on type interventions are usually implemented by civil society organizations who engage with the communities for a much longer time and work with them in overcoming the constraints imposed by specific inadequacies in agricultural skills, exposure, information, inputs, technology and market links.

The study groups tribal communities into three classes based on their livelihood patterns. The communities which have long experience and engagement in agriculture as well as a clearly articulated desire to intensify it with irrigation are termed agricultural tribes. Santhals of Bengal and Oraons, Mundas and Hos of Jharkhand, Gonds in central India or Bhils in western India perhaps illustrate this type. The communities which practice subsistence agriculture with high dependence on forests for supplementing their food requirement are termed as subsistence tribes. The Kolams and the Kols, Baiga Kondhs, yet, illustrate this category. Tribes, which have depended for a long time on artisan work or now have shifted to wage work are called wage-earning tribes. The study offers inferences as to which type of techniques and technologies are likely to work under what conditions.

The third pertains to gender impacts of increased water-use and agriculture intensification. The study (Marathe 2004) notes that even though the tribal societies have traditionally given a better status to women than their non-tribal counterparts, this does not imply the absence of male dominance among them. The study reveals that the absolute as well as relative work burden on women increases with adoption of intensive agriculture. While food intake of women also rises; they do not always get a proportionate share in the increased disposable income. The study also finds that the negative impact of such interventions seem to get reduced when these are coupled with other interventions such as women self-help groups.

Finally, the fourth study is devoted to discussion of emerging models that could conceivably reduce the burden on public systems. The burden of creating demand for water control strategies in social contexts of subsistence and non-agricultural tribes often falls on the intervener and this introduces delay in adoption of intensive agricultural practices. This study suggests experimentation with a model for 'service providers' (Mardikar 2004) who would undertake the associated tasks of demand creation and supporting water use as a means of livelihood. It suggests that a service provider equipped with multi-utility equipment such as power tiller could generate his own livelihood by offering services such as tilling, irrigation and transport, thereby also benefiting a large number of tribal users in energy-scarce eastern India. It disabuses the notion that each tribal family must own a pump for benefiting from water control and shows how the capital investment can be made viable for an individual entrepreneur while producing desirable social consequence. The study suggests a possibility of linking this model with the ABC (Agri-Business Clinic) model promoted by NABARD. However, this would require a few adjustments in the existing guidelines set out by NABARD for the ABC model. For instance, the existing NABARD guidelines require that the ABC entrepreneur must have a minimum level of formal education if this stipulation is removed, the tribal people in the region can benefit enormously.

To conclude this discussion, since the data on human development indicators has consistently pointed out a yawning gap between tribal homelands and national averages, attempts to redress the deficient public services naturally assumed priority. This perhaps explains the excessive concern of the tribal sub-plan with themes such as 'ashram shalas', curative health care and public distribution system. Yet, to accept the above as adequate explanation for the neglect of agriculture and water resources development in tribal areas perhaps would be naive. Water resources development in the country has for long followed the 'civil engineering' model of building dam and canal systems. Initial national concerns with food security needed creation of irrigation potential at the quickest possible pace. Since valleys offered the more easy work areas for this, the catchments-dam-canals model was widely used. This model is obviously not suitable for the tribal people. They usually live in uplands and upper reaches while gravity must make water flow to the valleys.

Even the model of groundwater development, which today is leading the agriculture development in several states of the country, seems to have bypassed the tribal people (Shah and Singh 2003). While the strong farmer lobbies in various states have been able to force the respective governments to adopt an extremely populist stance regarding electricity charges to suit the people who could not be reached through the canals, tribal farmers have not been able to extract similar concessions. In fact, a bulk of the eastern Indian tribal heartland have no power supply worth the name and in some places, it may take decades before electricity these regions. The results are quite clear for all to see. Wises abundant states such as Orissa and Jharkhand, which have the potential of becoming the largest exporters of virtual water provided the food and water resource development policies were designed in tune with water availability) to the rest of the county are also the most food insecure states and end up importing virtual water in the form of food grains from water–scarce regions of the nation. Almost all the cases of starvation deaths are reported from tribal areas: Kalahandi and Melghat in Orissa are the most frequently reported places for these tragedies.

The efforts on the part of the government have yielded some results. The Million Wells Scheme (MWS) of the ministry of rural development (MoRD) was an initiative targeted toward marginal and small farmers of SC/ST households. Concurrent evaluation of the MWS [Panchmukhi and Nayantara 2001] reveals that an additional area of 7,33,181 hectares has been covered by irrigation as a consequence of the scheme. The study concludes that by and large the MWS has benefited small farmers in the country; however the poorest may not have benefited as a result of the existing selection method, i.e. first come first served and high levels of political interference in this procedure. In another study [Janaiah et al 2000] carried out among tribal families in Chhattisgarh, it was found that the income from the crop in irrigated fields was almost 52 per cent higher than the income from non-farm activities such as fuel collection, grazing etc, and engage fully in farming. There is also evidence that despite charges of malpractices and implementation problems, intensive development of smallholder irrigation is ushering in a green revolution in Assam. Several other studies [Rayate 1989; Ramaiah et al 1991; Sharma 1998; Minj 1999] show similar results of water control interventions.

Even during the course of CInI studies, we found that wherever an intervention has helped to place improved water control in the hands of tribal farmers, many other changes have quickly followed culminating in improved income, employment, household food security and reduced distress migration the presence of other favourable factors such as market linkages, institutions for credit and input supply, extension and other technical support have helped magnify the beneficial impact. Hence, while improved water control alone may not address all the problems which the tribal people in central India face, it does have the potential to become the trigger which can place the tribal economies into an upward-ratchet of food security, reduced distress migration an better living conditions.

CONCLUSIONS AND SUGGESTED STRATEGIES

Regions and Approaches

Our research suggests a good fit between a set of contextual factors within an identifiable set of external constraints, and an identifiable portfolio of options for promotion of water control strategies. These contextual factors vary across the central Indian tribal homelands. The key factors pertain to agro-climatic conditions, location of a tribal hamlet in the local topography, level of infrastructure development and the social attributes of the tribal communities. We therefore use a combination of these to classify the central Indian tribal belt into four distinct socio-ecologies and suggest region-specific water control strategies for enhancement of tribal livelihoods. There are bound to be some overlaps in this broad classification. For example, Dangs in south Gujarat, which falls in Zone C, might better represent characteristics of Zone A while regions around Ranchi which fall in Zone A, but where exposure to settled farming is much greater, may represent Zone B. Hence, the zoning can better be seen with respect to the attributes rather than just the geographical locales.

The implementation strategy in a locale in any zone must naturally depend on the specific constellation of socio-economic and physical attributes prevalent in the locale. We believe that the above logic of attribute-based zoning offer useful guidelines in conceptualizing the local fully. The implementation strategy will be based on a logical choice of specific activities chosen form the portfolio of options for the concerned zone. It will also be fruitful to explore how the labour component of the activities can be paid for through a Food for Work mechanism. We also believe that irrespective of the zone, the basic principle will remain the same: initialize the tribal people in using water, helping them internalize simple water control techniques and skills for growing crops while giving full help in auxiliary inputs and then going in for capital intensive hands-off type components. As an illustration, we elaborate the strategies for one of the zones (Zone A) here.

Water Control Strategies for Zone A

The most critical issue facing this region is food insecurity arising out of unstable kharif crop. Paddy mono-crop dominates this region and because of a lack of water control and the fact that the tribal people in the region have not traditionally been exposed to settled farming, the paddy yields are quite low. Paddy instability arises from two factors and both these relate to the absence of water control. The first is the uncertainty in transplanting paddy from nurseries in the event of insufficient rains during end July to mid-August. This got exemplified in wide scale failure of the paddy crop in Chhattisgarh in 2001-2002 leading to an almost complete drought situation there. The second uncertainty arises from failure of September ('hathia') rains. This is experienced quite often in Jharkhand and Orissa and the result at low paddy yields lead to high food insecurity and forced migration.

Free grazing of animals in the psot-kharif season is a common facet in these regions and this is a n overwhelming externality that discourages an individual tribal farmer from attempting second crop even where access to water is not an issue. Virtually no water control measures that help farmers tide over the two periods of moisture stress have evolved or been implemented by public agencies. At present, the dominant irrigation intervention in the region is installation of small, group-based diesel lift irrigation (LI) schemes on streams and rivers. These schemes are largely used for irrigating the second crops as the pumps are almost useless during the kharif season due to the high rate of stream flow (leading to flooding of streams) and the huge amounts of silt being carried by these streams. The high cost of diesel based pumping schemes reduces the viability and acceptance of these schemes. We, therefore, feel that the primary objective any livelihood intervention in this region should be to stabiles the hair yields and incomes. This will, as first step improve the food security of the millions of tribal in the region. Moreover, it will reduce the tribal dependence on migration and will encourage them on agriculture-based livelihoods.

We would like to suggest four distinct stages for water-based livelihood promotion initiatives in this region: *(i)* the first stage should focus on stabilizing the kharif crops and incomes. This can be done through the creation of a plethora of decentralized water harvesting structures close to farms. These should be prolific and perhaps a structure may be created for every two hectares, preferable in a cascade; *(ii)* once the kharif crop stabilizes and the tribal farmers feel much more secure about their food availability, schemes that promote second crop cultivation will also find greater acceptance and could be promoted. However, an essential precondition for this will be large-scale promotion of 'adgharas' or 'Kanji houses' in blocks of contiguous villages to overcome the problems of free-grazing; *(iii)* As a next step, use of the water stored in these small water harvesting structures and available streams for second crops should be the focus of interventions. Lifting devices such as low-cost and high-efficiency Chinese pumps, Willard type kerosene pumps, treadle pumps and shared facilities such as those talked about by Mardikar (2004) under the agri-service provider model outlined earlier may be encouraged.

At places where wells exist, low cost micro-irrigation systems can be introduced to support women-managed vegetable cultivation in homesteads. Uplands may be to be taken up for soil water conservation measures and growing improved grasses, timber, host plants for silkworms/lac and fruit trees; *(iv)* Finally, agencies can focus on implementation of stream based large check dam-cum-lift irrigation and other irrigation systems. The Gram Bhagirathi Yojana, based on large structures on streams and bigger lifts, as is being proposed by the government of Jharkhand, will meet the case. The earlier phases will bring the possibility of agriculture being a superior option to migration to the forefront in the minds of the tribal farmers. Secondly, group dynamics are also likely to work better once the benefits are palpable and reachable. Successful implementation of these strategies would result in substantially higher farm incomes (and purchasing power) for the tribal farmers. This will also provide an impetus to the non-form economy and increased labour availability to the landless and sub-marginal farmers.

Obviously, there will be pockets within zone A where the local conditions would allow direct implementation of phase II or III or IV directly due to greater proximity to markets, infrastructure developments and experience of and exposure to settled farming.

Ways Ahead

The tribal heartland of central India must be seen as the next granary for the country. If the low-productivity agriculture in this region is to be systematically transformed into a vibrant, sustainable and intensive agriculture, it will produce sufficient food and fruits to contribute significantly towards food security of the country as a whole. This issue becomes even more important for national food security if we look at the negative rates of growth in yields in state like Punjab and Haryana (Gulati 2002; Chand 1999, Singh and Kalra 2002), which have been the handmaiden of agricultural growth in independent India. Carefully implemented and sustainable 'water control' interventions in tribal homelands will contribute food and fibre to a nation that enjoys only a temporary holiday from the rigors of national food insecurity (Bhalla, Hazell and Kerr 1999). Such a process will also transform lives of millions of tribal people and increase their own consumption, food security and perhaps induce a stable life pattern for them. The impact on contributing towards more sustainable and yet complete utilization of land and water resources will be an additional benefit.

Mere research does not, in itself, make a strategy. The lessons from the research need to be wisely and prudently woven with the art of the possible in the extant administrative and implementation mechanisms with the state. We recognize that the state machinery has greater competence and hence a bias towards 'blue-prints' and a 'hands-off' approach to programmes and schemes while the water control strategies thrown up by the research require a 'hands-on' approach and a fluid choice of techniques contingent upon the unique constellation of resource and social features of a tribal locale. The current order of governance does not leave much hope for adequate implementation of such an approach even if the state were to shed its preference for such an approach even if the state were to shed its preference for blueprint methods of spending large sums of money. We also recognize that the portfolio of options cuts across jurisdiction of several agencies of the state: water resources development, environment and forests, rural development and tribal welfare. Yet, we fear that the task might be too huge to be accomplished within the means normally at the command of civil society organizations working with external project funds. We thus hope that implementation mechanisms that can make a serious attempt at implementing decentralized water control strategies will emerge. This can happen only if there is wide scale recognition of the existence of the problem and a wide social mobilization required to correct the situation. What is perhaps called for is a large-scale collaborative effort between the state agencies and the civil society organizations in first understanding the complexity of the problem and in working together to evolve solutions using the portfolio of options suggested.

4

Sustainable Livestock Production in Semi-Arid Watersheds

Watershed development programmes while exhibiting significant impacts in terms of increased crop production and productivity, appear to have accentuated the inter-household inequities, by ignoring or sometimes negatively affecting landless and livestock, especially small-ruminant, owning households. Enhancing the production potential of a watershed for sustainable livestock production, would contribute to livelihood- and equity-enhancing impacts of the programmes. Appropriate policy and investment decisions are crucial to making this plausible.

Introduction

Watershed Development Programmes (WDPs) were conceived as tools for correcting the regional imbalances in agricultural development created by green revolution, through investments in soil and water conservation

(SWC) and natural resource management (NRM) in rainfed areas. The WDPs have evolved from being purely technically oriented SWC programmes to more integrated and participatory programmes aiming at NRM with organization of beneficiaries (watershed plus) and more recently targeting livelihood improvement (watershed plus plus). Though the rationale for WDPs has been to promote inter-regional equity, the impact of watershed investments on inter-household equity has turned out to be mixed. Though the overall impact of WDPs has been positive and significant (Rao 2000), increase in physical and economic access to groundwater (Chandrakanth et al 20204), landless and marginal households hardly benefited from watershed development, while the better off households located in downstream areas and with access to irrigation have benefited most (Farrington et al 1999). The availability of irrigation is central to increased cropping intensity, crop productivity, hence labour absorption and reduced migration (Shah 2001). With the focus of most watershed development projects on increased crop productivity, the inequities embedded in the distribution of agricultural land were only reinforced. Recent evidence points out that in many watersheds inequities increased, since for non-land owning and-well owning households access to drinking water, grazing lands and other natural resources decreased (Kerr 2002; Batchelor et al 2003).

It is increasingly being recognized that to increase the equity of watershed development, more attention has to be paid to livestock production, which is a major livelihood activity in most rainfed areas. In addition to providing income through animal and dairy sales, it has an important function for crop production by providing manure and draught power. Especially in the ecologically fragile areas of semi-aid watersheds, livestock makes an important contribution to the survival of the economically weaker sections (India Task Force 1987), small ruminants in particular playing an important role in ensuring rural livelihoods against drought (Pasha 2000).

Water and fodder are the most critical constraints for livestock development in semi-arid areas. Although in some cases WDPs have tried to improve biomass production on commons, in most cases livestock production has insufficiently been accounted for, missing out on important opportunities to improve the livelihood of the watershed poor. Watershed development appears to have even negatively affected livestock production: due to grazing restrictions on common lands, households dependent on small ruminants have in some cases been forced to migrate with their livestock and/or to sell it off. For large ruminant owners the effects were not so adverse: as these species usually depend more on crop residues and stall-feeding.

This paper will elaborate how the equity and sustainability impacts of watershed interventions can be improved by targeting investments to incorporate livestock production concern and by increasing the livestock production potential in semi-arid watersheds.

Livestock Production in Semi-Arid Watersheds

The predominant farming system in most semi-arid watersheds is the 'mixed crop-livestock farming system' under rain fed conditions, supported with limited irrigation from existing tanks, open wells of bore wells tapping the groundwater. Traditionally, livestock production played an important role in the rural economy of India's semi-arid zones (Walker and Ryan 1990). On an average, 15 percent of household income was derived from livestock production. For poor households, like landless shepherds and women, the importance of livestock production is much larger: 2/3 of the rural poor have livestock for income and drought insurance. Whereas landless and marginal landowners would mainly depend on goat and sheep, large ruminants were mostly held by landowners as the costs of maintenance were high due to fodder scarcity (Walker and Ryan 1990). The share of household income from dairy production in different land holding categories (Table 1) reveals the critical dependence of landless and small landholders on livestock for their cash incomes.

Table 1
Annual Household Cash Income by Source

(In Percentage)

Category	*Dairying*	*Crops*	*Others*
Landless	53.08	0.00	46.92
Marginal	30.14	46.55	23.30
Small	29.17	53.75	16.58
Semi-medium	26.25	58.98	14.76
Medium	25.33	62.77	11.91
Large	19.02	71.48	9.50
All	27.28	55.36	17.36

Livestock holding is more equitably distributed than landholding: marginal and small holders together owned over 67 percent of all milking animals in 1992. distribution of small ruminant, pig and desi poultry follow more or less the same pattern as in the case of bovine: 86.6 percent of sheep and goat, over 90 percent of pig and desi poultry are owned by the marginal/ small holders and the landless, with marginal holders alone accounting for nearly three-fourth of the desi poultry.

A desk study of livestock-environment interactions (LEI) in watershed by Mangurkar et al (2001) highlighted some important issues. They found support for the hypothesis that WDPs tend to charge the livestock composition (numbers, proportion of different breeds and species in their total population) depending on the restrictions on access to feed/fodder resources and, quantitative change in the type and availability of fodder. Based on the documented success stories of the WDPs with livestock component, the study concluded that WDPs with integrated livestock component strongly strengthen the crop livestock integrated mixed farming system, with a positive impact on the environment. The study supported the premise that introduction of practices such as stall feeding, prohibited access to grazing resources and declining traditional arrangement in WDPs do influence the promotion of natural regeneration, but tend to adversely affect the livelihoods of the resource-poor livestock owners. Lack of appropriate policies and approaches, adequate poverty focus and convergence of related sectors in NRM programmes are limiting the promotion and effective utilization of positive LEI.

As a follow up to the Mangurkar study, the International Water Management Institute undertook together with five NGO partners (Sampark, Samuha, Sevamandir, WASSAN and WOTR) and with the support of CALPI/SDC and LEAD-FAO, a study (here after referred to as the LEAD study) to identify, research and document livestock-environment-livelihood interactions in five watersheds in semi-arid India. The partners expressed a need to better understand the factors determining the livestock production potential in semi-arid watersheds and options for enhancing this potential. The LEAD study, therefore, focused on not only the inter linkages between livestock production, resource endowment and market conditions, but also on the management of resources and policy environment: since sustainable livestock production depends strongly on community organization and their capacity to manage the common resources. This paper will present some preliminary results of the study, and elaborate how watershed interventions can support sustainable livestock production in semi-arid watersheds.

The five watersheds chosen for the LEAD-India study provide a representative sample of the broad diversity of Indian semi arid areas and offer adequate opportunities for a special focus on studying the livestock-livelihood dependence of poor and landless women and men. Criteria for site selection were relative resource scarcity and economic integration, resource scarcity being estimated by average rainfall and economic integration by location and market access. Some general characteristics of the selected watersheds are presented in Table 2. In all five sites, investments were made by non-governmental and governmental organizations in SWC, reforestation, horticulture development and rainwater harvesting. Apart from Kosgi watershed, where investments mainly focused on horticulture development, tank maintenance sand groundwater recharge, in most sites some investments were made to increase biomass availability through

Reforestation, pasture development and plantation

of road sides, sala beds and bunds.

Hydrological and land use analysis employing GIS/ RS techniques has been used to explore the biophysical characteristics in relation to livestock management practices. For the socio-economic and institutional assessments, primary information regarding livestock and livelihood patterns, resource management and institutions was collected at the village/hamlet level in all the watersheds through focused PRAs and key informant interviews. These qualitative data were ranked by the partner organizations, using the methodological framework provided by quantified Participatory Analysis (QPA) (James 2003). Household level data was collected from a sample of 200 households in each watershed through questionnaire surveys. The results presented here mainly draw on the watershed and village level data and results.

PRELIMINARY RESULTS ON LIVESTOCK—ENVIRONMENT—LIVELIHOOD INTERACTIONS IN WATERHEADS

Water and Biomass for Livestock

WDPs geared toward improving agricultural productivity on rain fed lands have tended to relay on a range of SWC techniques including structural and vegetative barriers, field bunds, and check dams, as well as erosion control through gully plugs, etc. Widespread adoption of WDPs has altered the water balance generally in favour of the uplands but also in the form of increased groundwater recharge that is most evident in water table increases in the valley portions of the watersheds (IWMI 2003). Several studies by IWMI and partners have shown how the intensification of land use resulting from WDPs has increased the availability and utilization of runoff water and soil moisture in the upstream reaches, which in the semi-arid agro-ecosystems described in this paper has tended to result in diminished runoff flows to down stream users (whether tanks, irrigation reservoirs, etc.). A secondary dimension of increased water availability in upper watersheds is the relative availability for agricultural lands us soil moisture and runoff conservation for pasture and forest lands, i.e., water availability for biomass production. This latter element has crucial implications for livestock dependent populations. While large ruminants, particularly mulch buffaloes, remain dependent on irrigated fodder or crop residues, the small ruminants and to a lesser extent non-lactating or non-draft cattle remain heavily dependent on biomass produced on the common lands. This raises an important policy and management challenge vis-à-vis the relative investment (financial, government, NGO, or community management) in WDPs on private vs. common or public lands.

When livestock owners do not take part in the planning and implementation of watershed development, the direct benefits of increased biomass availability and access to common lands are not recognized as such. In 4 of the 5 LEAD watersheds however, livestock owning households did take part in watershed planning and implementation, placing biomass enhancement and pastureland productivity on the agenda of watershed interventions. Although grazing restrictions were imposed, clear agreement were reached on how the fodder produced would be shared. By investing in roadside plantations, fodder cultivation

Table 2: Some General Characteristics of Study Sites

Name of Watershed Village	*Babulgaon*	*Kanakanala*	*Kalyanpur*	*Kosgi*	*LadkiNadi*
District	*Ahmednagar*	*Koppal*	*Udaipur*	*Mahabubnagar*	*Jhabua*
State	*Maharashtra*	*Karnataka*	*Rajasthan*	*AP*	*MP*
Scale of watershed	4,875 ha	14,518ha	4,664 ha	3,587 ha	5,338 ha
Market integration	Good access	Remote	Remote	Good access	Remote
Average annual rainfall	430mm	499mm	584mm	739mm	1,024mm
Livestock intensity (ACU/ha)	1.30	0.91	1.74	0.72	1.12
SWC: proportion of treated area	24 %	43 %	44 %	56 %	90 %
SWC : average expenditure / ha (Rs)	6,800	2,600	5,500	3,600	3,300

and drought support the pressure on available resources was further reduced.

The above compares the different climatic and water resource characteristics of the five watersheds studied by IWMI and partners. Of the five, aridity (Difference between water inflow and outflow through natural loss) is highest in Kanakanala and is much lower in Kosgi and Ladki Nadi, where rainfall is higher. In all five watersheds rainfall is confined to 2-3 months a year. Only in Ladki Nadi and Kosgi are water resources sufficiently stored. This not only has a direct effect on the availability of water for livestock drinking, but water storage increases the availability of supplemental irrigation ofr crop production through the year. This enhances the crop residue viability for livestock feeding, besides the effects on biomass growth on tank and nala funds throughout the year. The variations in biomass availability rough the year and the strong correlation of the same with in fall and irrigation is illustrated in table 2, for Ladki Nadi 2001-02.

Plotting the biomass produced in the watersheds (from RS analysis) with the precipitation shows that biomass in Kanakanala structurally less while the other four watersheds do not differ such in the peak biomass availability. In Ladki Nadi, V Babulgaon Kosgi watersheds and increase in biomass availability from can be seen. However, these inferences have to be read the caveat, as 2001-2002 was a drought year.

The land use pattern, which influences the amount of biomass produced, in the five study watersheds is presented in the above-mentioned table. Kosgi, which is the smallest amongst the watersheds being studied, has the lowest proportion of cultivable wasteland and the highest cultivable area (94 per cent) that is actually cultivated. With the highest rate of irrigation, and groundwater depletion, a question about the sustainability of the resources utilization arises. With most of the lands in Kosgi and Kanakanala being cultivated and relatively lower amounts of common land available for grazing, there is higher pressure of grazing livestock on the available lands. With irrigation, the trend is to grow cash crops, which have limited/ no fodder value precipitating the fodder shortages. Even though the percentage of cultivable wasteland and fallow land is high in the other three watersheds, there is seasonal variation and based on climate. For instance this year Ladki Nadi received good rains. As a result, more than half the fallow land has been cultivated. Most of the water-lands in these watersheds are affected by erosion and grazing pressure.

The comparison of resource endowments between the watersheds provides an impression of the differences in their livestock potential. However, the potential does not depend on resource endowment alone; the socio-economic conditions and the external and local management of resource play a crucial role in determining the same. This is the case in Village Babulgaon watershed, where good livestock production support facilities allow marginal farmers to maintain intensive production systems. The socio-economic characteristics of livestock production will be elaborated in the following sections.

LIVESTOCK PRODUCTION SYSTEMS IN WATERSHEDS

Live Stock Holdings and Intensity

The livestock holding households range from around 30 per cent in Kosgi to 85 per cent in Kanakanala.

Poorer villages with less access to irrigation do have more livestock. In Kosgi, trends over the last 10 years indicate that livestock holdings have been greatly reduced, mainly because of increased migration and mechanization. A shift from cows to buffaloes and from sheep to goat has taken place. Fodder scarcity increased, s hardly any common lands remained (only the tank buds) and crop residues are used for compost. In VB abulgaon, large ruminants are mostly cross-bred cows, mainly for dairy production and consequently, there is widespread stall-feeding. Bullocks are also many, mainly for draught power, but the numbers are decreasing due to mechanization. There are twice as many goats as sheep, because of social preferences. In Kanakanala, goats and sheep are most popular, with few buffaloes. Large ruminants are reared for draught (hardly any mechanization) and manure, small ruminants for liquidity and insurance. Dairying is a limited activity, but increasing in villages close to the town. Kalyanpur has an average livestock holding of 5-6 animals per family. Each family owns a pair of bullocks since mechanization is low. Goats are also popular since the meat fetches a good price. Over the last decade there has been a great decline in livestock holdings, mainly because of drought and diseases. The differences between livestock population among villages in Ladko Nadi are large. Livestock population has reduced due to the fodder and drinking water shortages because recurring droughts.

It provides the livestock intensity in the five watersheds being studied. It appears that the livestock intensity (ACU/ha) is positively correlated with rainfall, except in case of Kosgi watershed. This is probably due to the higher extent of cultivated land in the watershed an non-availability of commons for grazing. The highest livestock holdings, both small and large ruminants per household, is encountered in Kalyanpur and Kanakanala, the watersheds with the lowest bio-physical potential corroborating that in highly fragile environments, livestock becomes the major source of livelihood.

Though there are huge differences in livestock intensities among villages in the watersheds, there is no definite trend in livestock holding patterns or density among villages located in various reaches of watershed. Similar is the case with treated or untreated village/areas in the watersheds. Statistical analysis revealed that there is no significant correlation between population and livestock intensity. There is however a significant inverse correlation between availability of arable land per household and l livestock intensity.

Feeding Systems

Generally in semi-arid watersheds India, free grazing and stall feeding are not mutually exclusive, but coexist with the relative importance varying depending on the cropping intensity; proximity to forests, wastelands, and fallow lands and access to markets for milk and fodder [Puskur 2002]. In all the watersheds studied, crop residues are an important source of fodder and their importance has increased. While small ruminations are all free grazed, there is partial stall-feeding for large ruminates, especially for lactating and draught animals.

The farming community balances the fodder demand supply gaps by followings a discriminatory feeding regime within their herds, the high yielding animals receive larger quantities and better quality feed stuffs; older and unproductive animals receive the poorest quality and subsistence rations; work animals are raised on dry fodder only, with concentrate supplements during the working season [Kurup 2003]. Home grown/bought crop residues and grazing on CPRs, are the universal treatments for all animals. There are regional and seasonal variations in the availability of the different feed and fodder and farmers' feeding practices take into account these variations in supply.

Market Access

Out of the five watersheds being studied, dairy production is taking place to a higher extend in Kosgi and VBabulgaon (both of which have access to chilling plants and milk route) and to a very small extent in Kanakanala and Ladki Nadi, two village each, which are closer to towns. This indicates that market integration is an important factor in developing dairy as an enterprise. While commercial livestock production, especially dairying, seems to be stimulated by market access and infrastructure, it has to be noted that the livestock intensity in general is influenced by the resource endowment. The market access appears to induce a charge in species composition of large ruminants and also the mulch animal breeds. In Kosgi there is a clear shift to buffaloes primarily to improve dairy production for the market and in V. Babulagao; about 78 per cent of the cows are crossbreds. In Kanakanala and Kalyanpur in most villages there is no improvement in large ruminate breeds, whereas in Kosgi and Ladko Nadi some households have improved breeds and in V. Babulgaon most households have improved breeds.

In Kosgi, the SHG membership seems to be positively correlated with livestock ownership: especially goats and buffaloes. SHGs are especially responsible for the increase in dairy production. In Kanakanala, though development of SHGs has improved access to credit, it is not very clear whether this has helped livestock production.

Trends in Crop and Livestock Production in Watersheds

Watershed treatments generally increase crop output and therefore output of crop residues. With watershed projects and shift in cropping pattern has also taken place, for low to high value crops or from mono to mixed and inter-cropping. An increase in the extend of irrigated area and the well command area, and also an increase in ground water table, ranging from 3 to 38 m in different watersheds have been notice. Beneficial impact of watershed programme on moisture availability has been observed [Ninan 1997]. In the study watersheds, 100 per cent of the sample villages reported an increase in productivity of both irrigated and rainfed crops. Seventy-seven per cent of the study villages reported increase in the cropping intensity and 50 per cent reported a small increase in the rabi cultivated. WDPs through improvement in soil moisture content generally tend to bring about an overall increase in biomass cover of the land, many of them edible to the species normally depending or grazing.

The cropping pattern in all the watershed villages has changed over the last decade or tow. Only about 24 per cent of the sample village reports no change, while in 8 per cent there is a shift towards more dry land cash crops and in 24 per cent a shift towards wetland cash crops.

It is felt that there has been a general decline in the quality and quantity of crop residues for fodder, especially so during drought years. While 35 per cent of the villages report improvement in the availability or crop residues for some households, 27 per cent report a decline in availability for most households in the village. As a result, the households have responded by decreasing their livestock holdings, but would like to acquire livestock again when the situation becomes comfortable. There is a large import of fodder from outside the watershed during drought periods.

The water harvesting structures thought not planned explicitly with a focus on livestock, have served the livestock drinking water purposes. In several places they eased the constraint of water on livestock production. While 31 per cent of the villages report shortages of livestock drinking water and conflicts with crop production during drought years 27 per cent report the same being true even in normal years. It has been observed on many areas that due to lack of water, and in some areas due of consumption of dirty water by livestock, there is high incidence of livestock diseases. It has also been pointed out that in many places farmers consider construction of farm ponds as failure since they may not be able to use such water for various reason Ramanna 1991] and for livestock consumption.

While drought support to livestock is provided in 54 per cent of the study villages in the form of either livestock camps or provision of drinking water, no support is available in the region.

Management of Biomass, Land and Water Resources in the Watershed

In semi-arid areas, livestock production depends crucially on common property resources, like forests, common lands and village tanks. Coordination of resource use is needed to ensure at they are used in a sustainable way. Over the last decades the management of these resources has been partly decentralized to local communities and user groups. In the study sites, in most villages with access to forestland, some form of joint forestry management (JFM) exists. The impact of this on availability of fodder and the usufruct rights often remain unclear. In all the study watersheds this poses a serious constraint to sustainable resource management since it obstructs investments in biomass generation.

In most villages where watershed development takes place, attention is paid to soil erosion caused by overgrazing on common lands. The grazing restrictions that are usually imposed to reduced the pressure one the land do not necessarily have to affect marginal, small ruminant holders seemed to prefer controlled grazing to open access, since the availability of fodder is increased. However, only in 16 per cent of the village does controlled grazing takes place. Establishing arrangements of controlled grazing to improve fodder availability on common lands could be an important instrument to increase the productivity of livestock in semi-arid watersheds.

WDPs invest part of the funds in local institution building and empowerment, to ensure that the enhanced resource based continues to be managed in a sustainable what after project more in local capacity building than GOs [Farrington et al 1999; Kerr et al 2000] this was seen in the LEAD study sites too. In all NGO villages, local institutions of NRM like watershed committees and forest committees were established. In non–NGO villages, few NRM organizations seem to function in an effective way: In 90 per cent of the villages the role of the panchayat raj institutions (PRI) in NRM was said to be non-effective.

Livestock-related institutions like dairy cooperatives and producers/reeders orgaisation, here exist do not play any significant role. Only in some case, JFM organizations and water users associations were functioning for the management of forestlands and village tanks.

Clearly, the establishment of an organization for resource management alone does not ensure that resources are managed in a sustainable way. When asked about their own perceptions, villages responded in more than 50 per cent of the cases that local NRM was poor. Only in 20.25 per cent of the villages are land, water and biomass resources apparently managed in a sustainable way, leaving substantial room for improvement if the positive impact of watershed interventions is maintanined.

Finally, for the management of biomass, land and water resources to be sustainable it is not only important to have established institutions, clear rules and a sound system of monitoring and control, it is crucial that the institutions for NRM function in a participatory and equitable way. If marginal households have no access to community decision-making or if the local rules and regulations affect certain households in a negative way, improvements in natural resource availability are likely to reduce equity and threaten the sustainability of resource use in the long run [Farrington et al 1999].

Although in four of the 26 villages local NRM institutions were said to function in an equitable way, in most villages few members still seem to take most decisions. If watershed interventions are to be equity- and livelihood enhancing, ensuring full participation, including livestock owners, is an important first step. After all, enhancement of livestock production and sustainable resource management cannot be imposed top-down: it is the community, which has to reach an agreement on how to make best use of the scarce resources that are there.

Policy Recommendations

Mangurkar *et al* (2001) found that lack of appropriate policies has constrained both the benefits and equity of livestock out-comes of WDPs as well as their contribution to poverty alleviation. The ongoing study reported in this section indicated that additional equitable benefits any be achieved through:

Inclusion of the crucial dimensions of livelihood dependence of poor on the livestock sector and the value of livestock assets in poverty reduction (especially small ruminants) in the watershed development strategy of the government.

Consideration of the access of poor and the backward region/villages to the infrastructure on livestock health services, marketing, breed improvement in the state policy.

Emphasis on developing common property resources, productivity enhancement activities including diversification of crop patterns, fodder production in such a way that they pave way for high value crop-livestock integrated mixed farming as an income generation activity in the rainfed areas.

Increased effort for controlled grazing and community management of common and revenue lands with clear usufruct rights regarding investments in biomass (roadside plantations, vagabonds, revenue lands, forests).

Assessment of livestock drinking water needs and incorporating livestock watering ponds/points into the design.

Inclusion of livestock holders using the tanks for drinking water for their livestock in water user's associations and making clear provision for drinking water for animals while deciding on the command area to be irrigated in an year from the tanks.

Resource scarcity in semi-arid watersheds may introduce tradeoff between livestock and crop development, between upstream and downstream users, or between free grazing and stall-fed livestock. Adequate consideration must be given to the sustainability of land and water use practices in order to ensure inter-generational equity.

Strengthening of RPI to Play More Effective Role in NRM

Delineation of clear methodologies fro action planning, good field examples of practice, resource material and appropriate administrative procedures — planning, monitoring, etc.

5

Tube Well Irrigation System in India

The key hypothesis of policy-makers during the 1980s was that raising tube well density would trigger agrarian upsurge in Bihar as it did in Punjab, Haryana and western UP. The state did record high growth rates of cereal yields during the 1980s higher than the national figures. However, this promising development could not be sustained in the 1990s, and cereal yields have stagnated since then. Based on fieldwork in eight villages of Bihar, the paper argues that, more than agrarian structure, the lack of adequate infrastructure and economic incentives has contributed to the agrarian stagnation in Bihar. The growth potential unleashed by the expansion of shallow tube well irrigation has been constrained by: *(a)* complete neglect of public sector investments in physical and institutional infrastructure, and *(b)* unfavourable output to factor price ratios.

Introduction

After century-longs stagnation, agriculture in eastern India experienced a turn around in 1980s with rapid groundwater development. Especially, West Bengal and eastern Uttar Pradesh performed very well with growth rates in production becoming as high as 4-6 per cent during 1981-82 to 1991-92. Agricultural production and productivity levels in the middle state Bihar also witnessed a growth higher than the long-term growth trend of the state [Pandey and Pal 2000]. Yet, agriculture in the state grew at a slower pace, over a smaller base, for a shorter time a after which the momentum was lost in spite of an impressive expansion of tube well irrigation.

This paper tries to explore the reasons for this relapse. The first section of the paper presents a review of literature available from the existing body of research on reasons for the persistent agrarian stagnation in eastern India. The second section explores the latest trends in tube well irrigation and discusses the structure of water markets and their productivity and equity implication based on data from a primary survey. The third section of the paper discusses various macroeconomic factors which limit farmers' ability to leverage the newly created pump capital to increase crop productivity and raise incomes. This understanding is based on the knowledge of larger reality of agricultural scenario in Bihar and observations from filed survey. The last and the concluding section discusses various alternatives for raising crops yield and farm incomes based on studies of well-performing farms in the region.

Empirical Evidences

The study involved an extensive review of literature available on issues of agrarian structure and production relations, agricultural growth, groundwater development and water markets in eastern India and primary data collection using focused group discussions and interview schedules.

The primary data were collected from field studies carried out in eight villages from six districts of Bihar in 2003. Two of our villages are from Nalanda and Bhabhua districts of south Bihar while the rest six are from districts, viz., Muzaffarpur, Saran, Gopalganj, Darbhanga and Madhubani in north Bihar. While Darbhanga and Madhubani are agriculturally least developed, Nalanda and Bhabhua are agriculturally the most developed districts. Muzaffarpur, Saran and Gopalganj fall in between these two extremes. This paper is an attempt to distill the lessons learned during the fieldwork in these eight villages and put them in perspective of the larger reality of agricultural development in Bihar.

Literature Review

Till 1970s, the literature from agrarian studies were dominated by discussion on issues related to agrarian structure and production relations, groundwater development through expansion of tube well irrigation and development of water markets became the thrust area after the pioneering RBI report on agricultural productivity in eastern India (RBI 1984).

Agriculture in Bihar has remained stagnant in spite of rich soil, abundance of easily accessible water and a rich peasant tradition. This stagnation has been ascribed to several factors including the state's colonial legacy (Bharadwaj 1993; Banerjee 2002; Mearns 1999; Baneree and Iyer 2002), ecological conditions (Ballabh and Pandey 1997; Ballabh and Sharma 19910), demographi pressure (Verma 1993) and most importantly, the land tenure system and the agrarian structure it supports (Bhaduri 1973; Prasad 1974). These factors are believed to have impeded the transition of Bihar's agriculture from a semi-feudal to capitalist production system-an essential condition for agriculture growth (Patnaik 1987).

Inequitable land distribution and perverse land tenure relations are considered to be the backbone of semi-feudal agrarian structure in Bihar and therefore comprehensive land reforms is suggested as the policy measure. Abolition of 'zamindari', redistribution of surplus land, tenancy reforms and land consolidation are four components of comprehensive land reforms (Ballabh and Walker 1992). Among all Indian states, land reforms have been worst failure in Bihar, even when it took the zamindari system in 1953. While West Bengal could accomplish tenancy reforms through operation Barga and UP had considerable success in land consolidation (Pant 2004) both projects were abysmal failure in cost of production in Bihar. Poor infrastructure and under developed primary agriculture Bihar. For all practical purposes, the state has almost given up on this project of land reforms. After the act for compulsory land consolidation was passed in 1956 in Bihar; only 3 percent of the total cultivated land was reported to have been consolidated till 1976 and in fact land consolidation department has now formally been abolished in the state (Wilson 1999).

Changing the structure of landownership proved to be difficult because the zamindari system was highly institutionalized and the dominant groups were very strongly entrenched in the state machinery itself. The political difficulties apart, Dandekar and Rath (cited in Bardhan and Rudra 1979) have argued that in an overpopulated state like Bihar, it is futile to try resolving the problem of rural poverty by re-distribution of land which is in short supply as this will have to be achieved by enforcing extremely low land ceilings which cannot be justified on sound economic considerations or rational calculations. Similarly, Hayami (1981) argued that in conditions of high and increasing population pressure on land, land reform is likely to be infeasible and futile without reversing the trend of increasing return from land relative to labour. He posited that the trend would continue as long as increase in supply of labour outpaces the increase in labour demand and hence the best cure to the growing poverty and inequality was to augment land by investing in irrigation systems and developing land saving and labour-using technologies. He considered the technocratic approach to be the only practical approach for agrarian transformation in this region; since land redistribution is extremely difficult both politically and administratively (Hayami 1981).

From Land to Groundwater: The Paradigm Shift

This has been the viewpoint of development economists, namely, Tushaar Shah and Richard Palmer-Jones also who argued that in rainfed low productivity agricultural system control over land and labour were the key and as a result inequitable land distribution has been at the core of the current outmoded agrarian structure.

However, in the modern land saving, input-intensive agriculture, access to capital holds the key to agricultural growth, while land has become less important. This is reflected in the declining share of land in the gross value of produce. But, eastern India suffers from severe capital scarcity and existence of monopolistic markets which exacerbate the existing inequality and reinforce the outmoded structure. Machine-reforms, where in the government would help the resource poor farmers and landless labourers to get ownership of agricultural implements so that the inequity in landholdings could be compensated by equity in access to groundwater and technology, can bulldoze the ossified agrarian structure and unfold a new era of rapid agricultural growth with relative equity and reduced poverty. They suggest a government supported and subsidized capital formation in private sector with special targeting on poor and landless to bring about the change.

This was in line with the key recommendation the widely quoted RBI report on eastern India (RBI 1984) which also stressed mainly on a machine based approach of exploiting region's abundant groundwater resources using shallow tube well technology to intensify irrigation and increase agricultural productivity, thereby reduction poverty. Rapid tube well capital formation through government subsidized projects like free boring scheme became the corner stone of public policy in Bihar as well as in other eastern states. This marked a clear shift in the policy focus from land-based strategies to water and machine capital-based strategy for agrarian change in the region. Unlike in the past, the tube well capital formation was encouraged mainly in the private domain and special targeted schemes like the million wells scheme were devised for small and marginal farmers of scheduled castes and scheduled tribes.

Evolution of rental markets in pumpsets (often called water market in irrigation literature) helped overcome the problem of lumpiness of investment and scale bias of the tube well technologies, earlier though to be the main problems in adoption of these technologies in Bihar and rest of eastern India having stamp size plots and high land fragmentation (Dhawan 1982). Water markets facilitated access to groundwater of even the small and marginal farmers. Rapid groundwater development took place in Bihar powered by both policy push and private initiative. Density of bore wells and pumping sets had registered an exponential growth over last two decades. Between the two minor irrigation censuses in 1986-87 and 1992-93, the pump density increased fourfold in Bihar. Primary surveys carried out in nine villages in six districts of Bihar in 2002 and 2003 suggest that the pump density has increased even more rapidly in the last 10 years after the latest minor irrigation census. The surveys suggest that the density of bore wells is much higher than the pump density. In fact in these nine survey villages there was one bore well for every 2.5 ha of cultivated area. Such high bore well density is a response to high and increasing land fragmentation in the state and this has been made possible by low cost of boring (Ballabh and Choudhary 2002) and portability do diesel pumpsets.

Water Market as an Embedded Exchange: Examining Polanyist Argument

Even though the density of groundwater extraction

measures (WEMs) has rapidly increased, the actual role and potential of this pump-led market based reform strategy to bring equitable growth in the precapitalist agrarian economy of Bihar has been questioned by many researchers for instance Wood (1995) Chakravarty (2001) and Wilson (2002). They have used detailed village studies to show how machine distribution has in fact increased the inequity and strengthened the vice grip (rent extracting capacity) of already dominant landlords. They argue that the rental markets for equipments are far from impersonal and context-natural as assumed in neoclassical economics. Wood suggests that exchanges in rural water markets have non-economics. Wood suggests that exchanges in rural water markets have non-economics motives and they are essentially linked to the social fabric and embedded in social relationships. The imperfect, socially embedded groundwater markets have functioned to reinforce rather than relax the dependence, constraining the opportunity for many small farmers with non-fovoured client status to increase their cropping intensity. As a productivity outcome, land is either increasingly coming into the hands of adequately capitalized farmers or its potential with the new technology is under–realized. Thus, these technological opportunities are social constrained to serve non-productive purposes.

This, however, does not seem to be true everywhere. In our survey, we found access to groundwater to be more equitable than the land distribution in Bihar. According to the last minor irrigation census (1992) 76.67 per cent of all mechanized shallow tube wells (STWs) in the state are owned by marginal and small farmers. This is such more than their share in the total cultivable land in the state. This was corroborated in a recent primary survey of 263 farmers carried out by IWMI in seven villages in six districts of the north and south Bihar. As evident from the table, marginal farmers in the sample had only 7 per cent of the total land cultivated by the sample but they accounted for 25 per cent of all pump-owner in the sample. If we take both marginal and small marginal and small farmer categories together, they have 55 per cent of all pumpsets while they cultivate only 25 per cent of the total land-owned while they cultivate only 25 per cent of the total land-owned by the sample farmers.

The IWMI survey showed that a significant number of the sub marginal category of farmers, having less than 0.5 ha of land, also owned pumpsets. Form the sample of 263 farmers, 32 sub-marginal farmers had nine pumpsets among them while in marginal category (0.5-1 ha land holding) 66 farmers had 25 pumpsets among them. Thus, a large number of pumps are now owned by small and very small farmers, who are compelled to sell water as irrigation surplus from their own fields is not enough to make the pump investment viable. They pump for profit and not power as suggested by Woods (1995) and Bubash (2000). These farmers resort to renting out pumsets to improve the capacity utilization which ensures assess to groundwater to even inadequately capitalized farmers. Interestingly, the analysis of sample survey data showed that even large farmers were selling water as much as the small and marginal farmers. The correlation between landholding size and hours of water selling per year was positive, though weak (r=0.18 and significant only at 90 per cent confidence level. This probably indicates increasing acceptance of water selling by even the well off section of the rural society in Bihar a change from the early days of groundwater development when it was a social taboo [Clay 1974 as cited in Mukherjee 2004 and Wood 1995].

Wood argues that quite like in canal irrigation, there are tail enders in groundwater irrigation also. The pumpset and boring combinations irrigate the land of pumpset owner first; close non completive kin second; favoured clients third; and then a nonrandom group of non-intimate others. These non-intimate others, who are generally the marginal and sub-marginal farmers of deprived castes, like tail enders in canal irrigation, have by design, more precarious access to pump rental services in availability, timeliness and price of water. This constrains their ability to rely the full potential of groundwater irrigation resulting in sub-optimal productivity outcomes.

Wood's analysis was based on detailed study of one village in Purnea: One of the most underdeveloped districts of Bihar. We made an attempt to test if it was true across different regions of the state and if the picture has changed over last 10 years since Wood did his study. We correlated total hours of pumping/ acre year of water buyers against their landholding size and found the correlation between the two variables to be very weak and insignificant. The scatter plot revealed that both very large farmers and very small farmers use much less hours of irrigation per acre of their net sown area than the small and medium farmers. The correlation was run again after excluding the large farmers (> 10 acres of land) from the sample and found that the correlation coefficient for this sample became moderately strong (0.525); positive and significant even at 99 per cent confidence level. This suggests that irrigation use intensity follows an inverted 'U' shaped pattern vis-à-vis landholding size. Small and medium farmers (cultivating 2.5 to 10 acres of land) practice the most input intensive agriculture while the sub-marginal and large farmers have diversified away from agriculture giving relatively lower attention to farming on their own land.

Wood's analysis of pumpset as an abettor of inequality is not acceptable for two reason; first, it was found that diesel pumps were the most widely distributed mechanical input across various landholding classes and castes in all the villages and second, no significant and systematic difference was noticed in the pump rentals paid by different categories of farmers. Also, none of the 129 water purchasers in the sample complained about any difficulty in accessing pumpsets on rent. This is the reason why except the severely waterlogged areas, almost all land cultivated by the sample farmers was irrigated.

Over the years as pump densities have increased, water markets have become broader, deeper and more efficient and monopoly rents have gone down significantly as is evident from the declining water to diesel price ratio in the area. For example, when Shah and a Ballabhy studied the six villages in 1995, diesel price was around Rs. 7.50-9.05 while water price ranged from Rs. 20 to 30. Seven years later, when one of the six villages (Nariyar) was revisited, it was found that while diesel price had increased more than threefold to around Rs 25 per liter, water price in the village had increased only twofold form Rs 22-25 to Rs 50 per hour. The water to diesel price ratio had declined form 2.80–3.18 to less than 2 now.

The timeline data on water to diesel price ratio in Table 4 of Shah and Ballabh (1997) study reveals that in 1990s, one rupee increase in price of diesel used to cause several times higher increase in pump-rent in the market. IWMI's field studies in Bihar suggest that the trend has now revised. Several water buyers admitted to us that pump rentals had now reversed. Several water buyers admitted to us that pump rentals had not increased as frequently as diesel prices after the recent enforcement of open market price regime on diesel. This indicates a significant increase in the buyer power in the market which might have occurred due to increased completion in the market induced by increase in pump density over last decade. It would be interesting to point out here the more than half of all pumpsets the sample selected (76 out 137) were purchased after 1995, the year when Shah and Balla carried their study in Muzaffarpur.

Groundwater Irrigation Intensity in Rice–wheat Systems

The irrigation pattern of pump-ones was compared with the of renters for paddy and wheat. The purpose of the comparison was to see if the differential pumping patterns had any significant impacts on the productivity outcomes. In paddy, the most important crop for Bihar, there was no significant difference between pump-owners and renters in terms of hours of pumping/irrigation per acre and crop yield. Also, the correlation between hours of irrigation/acre of paddy and the yield obtained was found to be weak and insignificant at the state level. This is understandable as rainfall in the survey year was timely and adequate. A recent collaborative study by Rajendra Agricultural University (RAU) and International Rice Research Institute (IRRI) in eight villages of north Bihar also showed similar results with irrigation coefficient being weak and insignificant in the production function plotted for paddy [Singh, Pris and Lusi undated].

In the case of wheat, a weak but positive and significant correlation was found between pump-ownership and hours of irrigation/acre provided to the crop. Hours of irrigation and yield were insignificant. A closer look at the date a suggested that though the incidence of pump-ownership was higher among the farmers in south Bihar, wheat yields were lower there.

This dichotomy was noticed during IWMI's fieldwork also. Famers in villages of south Bihar invest greater amount of resource and effort in Kharif crop while rabi crops were more important to the farmers in the villages of north Bihar. Separate analysis carried out for the four villages of north Bihar showed that yield difference between pump-owners and water buyers was small but significant at 95 per cent confidence level while the difference in hours of irrigation given per unit area of wheat was significant even at 99 per cent confidence level. Correlation coefficients between ownership and yield and ownership and hours of irrigation were also found to be positive and significant though quite weak (0.176 and 0.281 respectively). Except in case of wheat in the four villages of north Bihar, the results of our survey are similar to what Shah and Ballabh (1997) found in their study of six village in Muzaffarpur. Water buyers in IWMI's sample also use lesser hours of groundwater irrigation but use it more productively to reap same levels of yields as the pump owners.

Thus, it can be inferred that water markets have become more widespread and dense over the years facilitating almost universal access to groundwater in Bihar. Markets have also become more efficient as evident from declining monopoly rents over the years. Even though groundwater irrigation has become widespread and market exchanges have become more equitable, the intensity of groundwater irrigation has remained quite low. Farmers continue to economies on their irrigation cost which has risen sharply due to rise in diesel prices. The need for upfront cash payment for diesel pump irrigation also forces cash-starved farmers to under irrigate. The economization of irrigation cost is clearly evident from the annual pumpsage data of all categories of farmers in our sample. Three-fourths of sample farmers in Bihar provide less than hundred house of irrigation per hectare of their land under intensive rice-wheat cropping system. Assuming an average discharge of 35 m^3/hour, the depth of irrigation works out of be less than 0.35 metres for 71.3 per cent farmers. This is quite low for a double-cropped land even in a high rainfall area like Bihar. If we look at wheat, the main rabi crop in the state, it can be found that half of the farmers provide less than 50 hours of irrigation per hectare of their cropped area. This translates to an average irrigation depth of just 0.175 meters, which is much lower than the irrigation level recommended for the crop in the state.

This over-economy of groundwater use affects the yields of the crops received in the state and precludes further intensification of cultivation on land in spite of high population pressure. Almost three-fourths of farmers (72.56 per cent) receive less than 7 tonnes of cereal per hectare of net sown area. Combined yield of rice and wheat of one-fifth of farmers in our sample was less than a typical Punjabi farmer's rice yield alone. Accordingly, gross returns from agriculture are also extremely low. While one-third of farmers in the sample earned Rs. 25 to Rs. 30,000 per hectare of their net sown area under rice-wheat system, another one-third realized less the Rs. 25,000. Combined per hectare gross value of produce at farm gate prices was less than Rs 35,000 for 90 per cent of the farmer in the state. The average figure for the whole sample is around Rs 28,000/ha/year. Considering the land-man ratio of 12.78 persons/ha in rural Bihar, the gross value of produced/capital/year amounts to just around Rs. 2,000.

This is one of the important reasons for high incidence of rural poverty in Bihar, the only state in India where the absolute number of poor people below poverty line has registered an increase between the last two rounds of sample surveys of NSSO [Ahluwalia 2001].

Why Tubewell Irrigation Development Is Not Enough to Sustain Growth?

Agricultural growth remains low is Bihar in spite of increased pump density and access to irrigation. Growth fuelled by groundwater development has been short-lived and much less significant than that in the neighbouring West Bengal, Eastern UP and even Bangladesh with which it shares its history and ecology. Whatever production increase has been relished had been offset by population growth and as a result, per capita food availability and labour productivity have remained at the same level as in the 1960s.

What explains the persistence of agrarian stagnation

in Bihar in spite of rapid pump capital formation? Why have farmers in Bihar failed to leverage access to groundwater to increase productivity, intensity and income from agriculture?

Declining Output Price Ratio

This issue was raised repeatedly in focus group discussions with farmers during the fieldwork an din all the eight villages covered in the study the response was unanimous: sharp increase in diesel prices is the principal factor affecting agricultural growth. Today diesel has replaced muscle as the main motive power in agriculture and its rice has increased more than three times in last eight years (from 1995 to 2003) resulting in a corresponding increase in costs or irrigation, land preparation and threshing. Since diesel is available only on cash payment, there has been a substantial increase in the cash outlay of agriculture with increased dieselisation and rising diesel prices, resulting in a resource squeeze in these credit-starved village.

As subsidies were reduced, there has been a substantial increase in price of chemical fertilizers, For example, the retail price of urea remained stable at Rs 2.50/kg throughout the 1980s while in last 10 years the price has increased more than tow times to about Rs 5.30/kg. There has been a much steeper rise in prices of DAP and potash. Agricultural wages have also doubled up and between 1995 and 2003 and they have become progressively more monetize. There has been a sharper increase in peak-season wage rates than the non-peak season wage rates. Increased out-migration in peak seasons is cited as the reason for this increase even during a time when landowners' returns from agriculture has taken a beating.

Depressed food grain prices and absence of effective price support were also considered to be equally responsible for agricultural stagnation. It was pointed out that while cost of all inputs has increased manifold, food prices have gone down in real terms. The average farm-gate price of paddy and wheat has hovered around Rs. 350/quintal and Rs. 525/quintal respectively in the last three seasons. The harvest price of paddy is lower than even its C^2 cost of cultivation as estimated by Commission of Agricultural Cost and Price (CACP) let alone the minimum support price offered by government of India.

Post 1991 increase in oil prices, reduction in subsidy on dies and fertilizer and slackening food prices in both national at international markets have together created a situation where terms of trade have regressively moved against agricultural and the profitability of food production has gone down spite of a modest increase in crop productivity in Bihar According to Hariss (1993), it was favourable factor primary ratio (In conjunction with availability of a new high yielding variety of rice (IR 36) that facilitated agricultural take-off West Bengal. Now, depressed food grain prices and increased of cultivation are producing a v\reverse effect, suppressing farmer margins and motivation to intensify inputs in agriculture, reusing in relapse of stagnation in state in late 1990s after a should period of growth in the 1980s. Similar problems have been reported in Bangladesh also when rise in diesel price following the Gulf war resulted in a fall in boor production in subgenus year [Palmer-Jones 1999]. Decline in rice price-fertilizing price ratio has been associated with slowdown in agricultural growth in Bangladesh [Shababuddin 1999] and Assam [Hussain and Kalita 2004]. In an analysis of slowdown of agricultural growth in Bangladesh, Palmer-Jones (1999) posits that the of rice prices in relation to agricultural input prices including agricultural wages have been an important determinant of agricultural growth.

Decapitalisation of the Rural Areas

Reduced rate of public capital formation and virtual collapse of infrastructure (such as rural roads, power supply, major and medium irrigation systems, sugar mills, etc.) has further worsened the situation. Empirical results for a period 1980-98 of an all India level study suggest that gross domestic product of agriculture (GDPA) is strongly influenced by: *(a)* capital formation in agriculture; and *(b)* terms of trade [Gulati and Bathila 2001]. Traditionally, public capital formation in agriculture in India has been mainly in form of major and medium irrigation systems, whereas in the 1970s and 1980s the focus shifted towards expanding well irrigation by providing increasing amount of electricity to agricultural sector [Dhawan 1996].

In the last two decades, public capital investment in agricultural in Bihar has concentrated mainly in increasing the density of shallow tube wells and pumpsets through credit and subsidy schemes like Free Boring Scheme, Million Shallow Tube well Project, on-farm Water Management Project, IRDP loans, etc, However, performance in major and medium irrigation systems and rural electrification which would have given long-term cost advantage to farmers in the state has been miserable. The actual irrigated area by major and medium schemes has gone down from 2.15 million hectares in 1990 to 1.58 million hectares in 1997 [Sharma

1998]. Nearly 21,000 villages are yet to be electrified in the state, while by Bihar State Electricity Board's own admission, 18,000 of the electrified 47,000 villages have come de-electrified due to various reasons. The per capita annual power consumption is as low as 22 kwh in north Bihar and 87 kwh in south Bihar [Sharma 1998]. Thus, when private cost of irrigation was falling in other states of India on account farmers in Bihar incurred increasingly high cost for irrigation Poor infrastructure means inefficiencies and higher costs of production Marketing. Storage and processing making agriculture nuncupative in the state.

Absence of the New Agrarianism in Bihar

Some researchers argue that phenomena like rapid decline in rural infrastructure, absence of procurement support and poor performance of rural credit schemes may well be the problems of demand rather than supply [Wilson 1999 and Shah, personal communication]. Kalpana Wilson argues that de-electrification and stage apathy by themselves cannot explain the stunted growth of capitalism in Bihar. Faced with similar problems, farmers in other parts of country have responded very differently. Remunerative prices, reliable power supply, free electricity and writing off of farm loans have been the rallying points of peasant movements in the capitalistically developed rural areas of the country like western UP, Punjab, Haryana, Gujarat, Maharashtra and Karnataka where peasants of varying economic status came together to extract concessions from the state [Gail Omvedt quoted in Hariss 1992]. This marked a clear shift from the historical pattern of peasant movements, which had almost always targeted at intra-rural class relationships [Hariss 1992]. But there has been complete absence of any such movements in Bihar, which shows a lack of demand for such services even if the need is not lacking. Wilson (1999) argues that this is mainly because the peasant capitalist development which started in parts of Bihar under favourable conditions of 1970s and 1980s could not be supported by the underlying agrarian structure and the nature of the state.

Towards Breaking Agrarian Impasse

Input intensification for improving efficiency and Income: A Possible Option for Rarmars.

With all these structural and macroeconomic constraints facing agriculture in Bihar, what are the options available for an individual farmer to expand his production and profit margins?

To understand this, an analysis of best practices in agriculture was carried out in one of our study villages, in which the agricultural practices and crop-economics of a small group of farmers who achieved the highest productivity levels were studied and compared with that of the modal group of farmers. The comparison revealed two important pints. First, the yield obtained by most of the farmers was just enough to cover their input costs and there was hardly any surplus left even for consumption, let alone capital formation. This resulted in continued poverty and stagnating of agrarian economy. Also, with just 28 per cent. This means that most of the farmers in Bihar are practicing what Tushaar Shah calls cost-covering agriculture' and from this point if the crop yields are raised even by 20-25 per cent, the net incomes of farm households would increase by 60-70 per cent making a significant dent in rural poverty in the state. Second, farmers who made more intensive use of inputs and incurred higher cost s towards cultivation were more efficient and competitive producers with much lower per quintal cost of cultivation. This shows that input intensification to increase yields is one possible way of reducing per quintal cost of production and increasing profit margins. IWMI research in north China shows that it is through relentless intensification and raising crop yields that Chinese farmers have retained the viability of their farming in the face of declining global food grain prices and rising input costs and local taxes [Shah, Giordano and Wang 2004].

This strategy, however, will catch on only if production and price risks are low and farmers have access to suitable crop varieties which respond adequately to input intensification. Paddy crop faces risk from flood in large parts of north Bihar. Lack of suitable varieties for poorly drained low lands called churns which form a significant proportion of the total cultivable land in the region is also a big stumbling block. This is the reason why south Bihar where problems of flood and drainage are not very serious (except in Mokama Tal) level of input use in paddy and is yields are much higher when compared to flood-prone north Bihar.

In case of wheat, the main rabi crop in Bihar, almost all our respondents complained that the crop was not very responsive to input intensification and seed up-gradation. Agronomists agree to this point. The problem lies in the late sowing of wheat in Bihar which forces early maturity, resulting in lower yields. Field experiments carried out by the ICAR scientists in Directorate of Water Management Research, Patna have shown that one month delay in wheat sowing from its recommended time of November 19-25 results in about 53 per cent reduction in yield [Singh et al 2002]. Such delay is common in Bihar and in fact in many areas the sowing goes on till as late as second week of January. Late sowing and hence late harvest of paddy crop cause the delay. At present farmers wait for monsoon rains to sow paddy and transplantation is carried out generally in the third seek of July. ICAR studies show that advancing sowing of rice by a month will help to realise higher yields of both rice and wheat. However, this requires irrigation for the crop in pre-monsoon period. Therefore, increasing groundwater use is still the key to agrarian development in Bihar [Singh et al 2001]. Prohibitively high cost of irrigation is the biggest hurdle in large-scale adoption of this proven strategy of yield enhancement in rice-paddy systems of Bihar.

Policy Choices for State

Rural electrification is one state initiative, which can provide major boost to agriculture in Bihar. It can bring down the cost of irrigation and improve the working capital situation of farmers. It can also trigger growth in storage and processing infrastructure, which will permit value addition and the much needed crop diversification in the state. Cheaper access to irrigation with electricity will also encourage farmers to bring larger areas under summer crops where higher yields can be obtained under more controlled conditions.

Behaviour of producer prices has been another important impediment to agricultural growth in Bihar. The high level Committee Report on Food Policy notes that the producer prices were higher in this region than Punjab-Haryana in the early 1980s but became lower in the early 1990s as surpluses appeared (http://fcamin.nic.im/hlc_contents.htm). The combined pressure from subsidized sales by Food Corporation of India (FCI) under its Open Market Sales Scheme (OMSS) and local seasonal gluts results in producers getting prices well below the actual economic cost of production in Bihar. Poor infrastructure and under-developed primary agricultural marketing network further worsen the problem of farmers by increasing the cost of marketing and price fluctuations. Unless this is addressed by extending procurement operations more effectively in the state, there will be insufficient incentive for the sustained yield increased.

6

Water Trade and Water Productivity

During the past 50 years, Gujarat has led India's exemplary growth in dairy production by forging the world's best-known cooperative movement. Thanks to the market access and production enhancement programmes run by cooperatives, dairying has emerged at the centre stage of rural livelihoods systems in arid and semi-arid regions. However, intensification of dairying has been accompanied by intensive use of water used in growing feed and fodder. This study estimates that dairying-based rural livelihoods systems are now threatening the limited water resources of arid and semi-arid areas, and their future in turn is threatened by the depletion of these resources. The paper analyses virtual water exports and imports by some of the leading dairy cooperatives of Gujarat.

Introduction

With the advent of green revolution technologies and water-intensive crops, the pressure on groundwater for irrigation has enormously increased in Gujarat (Bhatia 1992). Decline in groundwater levels leading to increase in cost of water abstraction structures in depriving resource poor, small, and marginal farmers of direct access to groundwater. Those, whose wells have dried up, largely depend on water purchased from rich well owners often at prohibitive prices to sustain irrigated agriculture (Gass et al 1996; IRMA/ UNICEF 2001). To cope with the situation, farmers are shifting to low water-intensive crops having high economic value (Kumar 2000, Kumar forthcoming). Farmers are also switching from crop production to dairy production given the shot-term cash flow and stable income from it. The dairy industry has seen a major upswing after the inception of 'Operation Flood Programme' in India, which was launched by the National Dairy Development Board, Anand in 1970. India has emerged as the largest producer of milk in the world by attaining 81 million tonnes during 2001 (Singh and Pundir 2003). Gujarat is one of the fore runners of dairy production in the country. But this changing trend has added to the burden on already stressed groundwater resources.

Dairy farming involves not only direct consumptive water use by cattle for milk production, but also embedded water in green fodder and byproducts of cereal crops and other cereals and crop residues that are fed to cattle. Dairy farmers in Gujarat are heavily dependent on import of dry fodder and feed, which points to growing trade in 'virtual water' (Allan 1993).

Virtual water is defined as the volume of water required to produce a commodity or service (Allan 1998; Hoekstra 1998). It has also been called 'embedded water' (Hoekstra 1993). The transfer of virtual water embedded in various commodities and services that are traded is becoming an important element of water management discussions at global as well as regional level, particularly in regions which experience water deficits for food production (Chapagain and Hoekstra 2003). Chapagain and Hoekstra (2003) have developed a methodology to quantify the virtual water flows between nations through trading of livestock and livestock products. According to their estimates, global virtual water trade through crop and livestock products is estimated to be 940km^3/year, equivalent to a quarter of India's annual precipitation. Livestock and livestock products accounted for 26 percent of this trade.

A dairy animal requires only about 70 and 80 litres of water per day in the form of drinking water. Lactating dairy animal requires some more water to produce milk (2.5litres drinking water per litre of milk production). A cow or a buffalo producing 10 litres of milk a day, then, would require about 100 litres of drinking water (Trivedi, personal communication, 2003). But this only the tip of the iceberg so far as water use in dairy farming is concerned. Singh and Kishore (2003) found that average daily water used by buffalo and crossbred cow in Mehasana district of Gujarat was 10.18m3 and 10.51m3, respectively, with the share of drinking water being less then 1 percent, while embedded water accounts for the rest.

Main Contents

The objectives are to: *(i)* quantify the total irrigation water used for crop and dairy production in different region of Gujarat, and disaggregate water use in dairy production for buffalo, crossbred cows and indigenous cows: *(ii)* estimate the irrigation water productivity of crop and dairy production both in agronomic and economic terms; & *(iii)* quantify the virtual water trade through trading of milk in different region of Gujarat.

The study covered five district cooperative dairy cooperative unions falling in three distinct regions of Gujarat: *(a)* Anand and Surat districts dairy unions in south and central Gujarat; *(b)* Mehsana and Banaskantha districts dairy unions in north Gujarat; and *(c)* Rajkot district dairy union in Saurashtra region. Two villages were selected from each union and from each village a sample of 30 dairy farming households was surveyed.

Mehsana and Banaskantha fall in the north Gujarat region, which is 'absolutely waterscarce' going by Malin Falkenmark's index of physical water scarcity (IRMA/ UNICEF 201). Rajkot district falls in Saurashtra, which according to the same index is a 'water scarce' region. Anand and Surat fall in south and central Gujarat, which is a 'water abundant' region (ibid).

The study considered both direct consumptive water use and embedded water use (irrigation water used for producing inputs of dairy production) to estimate total water used for dairy production. The estimates understate true water use because all calculations are done for irrigation water use; the use of rainfall and soil moisture is excluded. Throughout the paper then by 'water productivity', we mean 'irrigation water productivity'.

During 2000-01, total milk production in the state was 53.13 lakh metric tones and it accounted for 6.57 percent of India's milk production. The per capital milk availability was 294 grams/day and is higher than the national average and also the nutritional requirement recommended by the Indian Council of Medical Research, i.e., 250 grams/capita/day. Continuous and rapid growth in dairy production in Gujarat was achieved through increase in holding of improved cattle breed, increase in use of balanced cattle feed, and improved veterinary services. Another significant important input of dairy production was expansion of irrigated fodder crops. The contribution of irrigated area under fodder crops to gross cropped area is presented. The contribution of irrigated area under fodder crops has declined in south and central Gujarat during 1975-76 to 1995-96, whereas significant increase in the area under fodders is observed in north Gujarat and Saurashtra region during the same period of time.

The survey data on the average depth of irrigation water applied by farmers to major crops and their allocation between main and byproduct. We allocated the total water used between main and by products according to he ratio of income from the main and byproducts (Dhondyal 1987). Alfalfa is one of the important green fodders and is being grown by dairy farmers in all regions. Average depth of watering for alfalfa varied from 1,080 mm (in south and central Gujarat) to 2,079 mm (in north Gujarat). Dairy farmers are growing maize as a green fodder across the study area and its average depth of watering varied from 274 mm (Saurashra region) to 948 mm (north Gujarat). Sugar cane and tobacco are important among cash crops which farmers in south and central Gujarat grow. Sugar cane is more water-intensive compared to tobacco. In Saurashtra, highest water use occurs in cotton and the lowest in kharif groundnut. Among foodgrain crops, wheat is grown all over Gujarat and the depth of watering applied in it varied between 634 mm (in Saurashtra) and 919 mm (in north Gujarat).

Season wise average daily feed and fodder input to in-milk and dry animal and calf were estimated first using our survey data; using average daily feeding pattern, these values were imputed into the entire life cycle of the animal. Based on these, the daily inputs of dairy production were estimate. In south and central Gujarat, of average daily fodder fed to dairy animals, large share comes from the local grasses, whereas bulk of the dry fodder fed is paddy straw. In case of concentrate, large portion comes through balanced cattle feed ('Amuldan/Sumuldan'). In Saurashtra region, large share of greens comes from maize fodder; while the most popular dry fodder in the region is groundnut straw. Balanced cattle feed ('Rajdan') and cottonseed cake are used as concentrates. Dairy farmers of Saurashtra breed the indigenous 'Gir cow', known for its endurance and relatively higher milk yield when compared to other nondescript cows. In north Gujarat region, alfalfa is a preferred green fodder; bajra and jowar straw are the main sources of dry fodder. The concentrate is given in the form of balanced cattle feed ('Sagardan'/'Banasdan') and cottonseed cake. Across the regions, almost the same quantum of green and dry fodder is fed to in-milk and dry animals.

However, the concentrate is fed only to in-milk and pregnant cows and buffaloes in advanced pregnancy.

In south central Gujarat, average daily milk production of buffalo and crossbred cow were estimated to be 1.87 litres and 2.90 litres per animal, respectively. Average daily milk production in Saurashtra region for buffalo, crossbred cow and indigenous cow are 4.72 litres/animal, 6.39 litres/animal and 4.08 litres/animal, respectively. For north Gujarat region, it is 3.82 litres/animal, and 4.00 litres/animal for buffalo, crossbred cow, and indigenous cow, respectively.

With shorter inter-calving period, less time to arrive at first calving stage and longer period of lactation, the average daily milk production of crossbred cow is more than that of buffalo and indigenous cow. Interregional variation in productivity of crossbred cows is probably explained by the differences in relative importance of dairying in the livelihoods. In water abundant south and central Gujarat, crop production is the main source of livelihood but in water scarce north Gujarat and Sourashtra, dairy farming is the primary source of livelihood and crop production is secondary.

The above paragraph presents the physical, net, and gross value productivity of major crops grown cross the three regions of Gujarat. Physical productivity is crop yield per unit of irrigation water (kgs/m^3), whereas value productivity is the value of output per unit of irrigation water (Rs/m^3). The physical and gross value productivity of water in alfalfa was found to be the highest in south and central Gujarat and lowest in north Gujarat. Dairy farmers grow maize as a green fodder across the study area and physical and value productivity of water in maize production was highest in Saurashtra region and lowest in north Gujarat farmers grow sugar cane and tobacco, and gross value productivity of water in tobacco was found to be higher than that of sugar cane. In Ṣaurastra region, value productivity of irrigation water was the highest for kharif groundnut and lowest for cumin. In north Gujarat, cotton, Castor, and mustard are the main cash crops and net value productivity of water is the highest for green gram and lowest for seasamum.

Among foodgrains, wheat is grown across all the three regions of Gujarat under study, and gross value product of water use in wheat is lowest in north Gujarat and highest in Saurashtra. The net value product of water in paddy is estimated to be Rs. 0.20/m^3. In north Gujarat region, farmers are growing bajra and jowar during both kharif and summer season. The net value product of water in kharif bajra and summer bajra are Rs.0.64/m^2 and Rs. 0.62/ m^3 respectively

Water Used in Dairy Production and its Productivity

In this section, we present the estimates of the amount of embedded water in the feed and fodders of different types of cattle on the basis or irrigation water applied. The daily direct (drinking water) and indirect (water used for feed and fodder production) water consumed by different types of animals across the regions of Gujarat. The share of drinking water is less than 1 percent of total water used by dairy animals.

In south and central Gujarat, embedded water use is the highest in the form of concentrate feeds, followed by green and dry fodder. The physical and net value productivity of water in milk production for crossbred cow is more than that for buffalo. In Saurashtra region, daily water used for milk production, highest portion of embedded water comes from concentrate followed by green and dry fodder. The physical product of water in milk production is highest for indigenous cow and lowest for buffalo, whereas net economic efficiency of milk production is highest for buffalo and lowest for indigenous cow. In north Gujarat region, of the total water used for milk production, largest share comes in the form of green fodder followed by concentrate and dry fodder. The physical and net value productivity of water use in milk production is highest for crossbred cow and lowest for indigenous cow.

Normally farmers do not consider those inputs which are already available with them either as byproducts of crop production or fodder produced in their farm. They consider only those inputs, which are purchased from the market. Secondly, farmers do not consider the 'virtual water', which comes from outside of the region in form of cattle feed. For calculation of water productivity in dairy production, we considered water used for green fodder production, ingredients of concentrate, which is produced within the region and drinking water. The water productivity in dairy production for the crossbred cow is higher than that of buffalo and the indigenous cow in south and central Gujarat and north Gujarat, whereas, in Saurashtra region it was highest for indigenous cow. It is important to note that in Saurashtra region dairy farmers prefer the Gir breed of cow, as it is more efficient in dairy production than the indigenous cow.

Alfalfa is a highly water-intensive crop, though the water requirement varies from region to region. Out of the total green fodder, share of alfalfa for different types of animals varies across regions. It is quite low in south and central Gujarat at 5 percent to 10 percent, whereas, in Saurashtra region, it is 22 percent to 28 percent and in north Gujarat region, it is as high as 34 percent to 46 percent. In north Gujarat, annual groundwater draft is about 1,528.8 million cubic meters (mcm)/ annum. Out of this alfalfa, alone takes away about 13 percent (198mcm/annum) of the total water diverted for irrigation (IRMA/UNICEF 2001). In north Gujarat, if we could cut down water application rate or increase irrigation water productivity of alfalfa, then it would help in making dairy production less water-intensive and will lead to substantial reduction in ground-water draft.

Kumar et al (2003) studied the performance of drip irrigation in alfafa cultivation in Banaskantha district of north Gujarat region and found that it could save about 43 percent irrigation water and increase the crop yield by 10 percent. The dairy unions of north Gujarat are major stakeholders in milk procurement and are constantly striving to increase their milk procurement from dairy farmers through promoting improved technologies for improving feed energy conversion efficient such as chaff-cutters and urea molasses block (UMB). Emerging research suggests that milk unions need to seriously consider programmes to motivate dairy farmers to adopt water-saving technologies, if necessary by providing credit and subsidy support to them. Doing this makes sense not only from the viewpoint of improving their business but also in terms of managing the precious groundwater resource which is so crucial for sustaining dairy industry in north Gujarat.

Virtual Water Used in Daily Feed Regimen of Cattle

In dairy production process, huge quantity of embedded water is traded in the form of dry fodder and concentrates. We have considered only the embedded water in the cattle freed, which is traded between the regions of Gujarat and between the states. The contribution of imported virtual water used in milk production per day per animal across the regions of Gujarat with different types of animals. The virtual water consumed by different types of animals depends on the amount of cattle feed fed to them. Buffaloes consume larger amount of virtual water as compared to crossbred cow in south and central Gujarat. In Saurashtra region, it was the highest for crossbred cow as compared to buffalo and indigenous cow, whereas in north Gujarat indigenous cows consume more imported water than buffalo and crossbred cow.

In the methodology we have used, the virtual water content of milk is the total water used for milk production. Based on this notion, our study makes an attempt to quantify the annual virtual water trade that takes place by the dairy unions in the form of liquid milk export outside the district/region and the import of balance cattle feed or inputs for producing balanced cattle feed form outside. For estimation of virtual water import and export, five-year averages of milk export and cattle feed inputs imports by the dairy union have been considered. We assumed that total raw milk procurement by union minus raw milk sold within the district was the net milk export outside the district. Then we derive,

Milk Export by Dairy Union

= Milk procurement – milk sale within the district Net virtual water export

= Gross virtual water export (milk)- Net import of inputs of cattle feed

First of all we considered the ratio of milk of buffalo, crossbred cow, and indigenous cow into total water used to produce that quantity of milk was estimated by multiplying the water used for producing a liter of milk by dairy animals across the dairy unions.

As per our estimate, the Anand dairy union exports 642 mcm of embedded water every year in form of milk procured by the imports. 93.67mcm/year embedded water in form of ingredients of balanced cattle feed. The net virtual water export by Anand milk union is a net importer as its total milk procurement is consumed within the district itself. The net virtual water import by Anand milk union is about 491.59 mcm / annum. The Surat dairy union is a net importer as its total milk procurement is consumed within the district itself. The net virtual virtual water import were 55.65mcm/year in the form of cattle feed. Surat, which falls in a water abundant region of south Gujarat, imports virtual water through cattle feed imports. In the case of Rajkot dairy union, the gross virtual water export is about 24.85mcm/year against virtual water import of 3.1mcm/year in the form of cattle feed from Meshana dairy union. The net virtual water export is about 21.84mcm/year. The gross virtual water export by Meshana dairy union is 1,311.49 mcm/ year while it imports 74.5mcm/yearinthe form of ingredients of cattle feed. The net virtual water exports 1,237.9 mcm/year while it imports 74.5 mcm/year in the form of ingredients of cattle feed. The net virtual water export is 1,237.09 mcm/year. Similarly, the Banashkantha dairy union exports were 913.43 mcm/year of virtual water against an import of 34.47 were 913.43 mcm/year of virtual water against an import of 34.47 mcm/year. The net virtual water export by the Banaskantha dairy union 878.96 mcm/year. Thus, north Gujarat, which is the most water scarce region of the state, exports the maximum quantity of virtual water (2,116.05 mcm) through its dairy industries.

For the purpose of quantification of total water used by dairy farming in the state, we collected district wise milk production by different types of animals for the year 1998-99 (GOG Undated). We have assumed that: *(i)* water used by different types of animals to produce one liter of milk in Kachchh region is similar to that in Saurashtra region; *(ii)* in south and central Gujarat, indigenous cow consumes same amount of irrigation water as a buffalo of same region is consumes.

Total milk production of the state during1998-99 was 4,843.84 thousand tones. Out of this, 28.54 percent milk was produced by non-descript and indigenous cows, 5.93 percent by crossbred cow, and 65.53 percent from buffaloes. From our survey, we know the estimated total water used to produce a litre of milk from different types of dairy animals in different regions. To quantify the total water used for milk during 1998-99, we multiplied total milk production by water used for a litre milk production. Based on the average figures of water intensity of milk production for different types of dairy production. Based on the average figure of water intensity of milk production for different types of dairy animals in different regions, the total amount of milk produced from these regions and its composition, the irrigation water use for dairy farming was estimated. The estimated irrigation water use to produce 4,843.84 thousand tones of milk by different types of animals (buffaloes, crossbred cows, and indigenous cows) in the state is about 14.96 BCM. It is important to point out that this estimate is based on the assumption that purely rain-fed milk production is insignificant in Gujarat.

7

Value of Ground Water

A study carried out in four villages in Banaskantha district of Gujarat estimated that 60 percent of that farm output generated through groundwater use in agriculture came from dairying. Tube well irrigation supports three-quarters of the farming household income in these villages and, strangely, this share is larger for water buyers and farm labourers than for tube well owners. This is despite the fact that tube well irrigation costs have soared rapidly with depleting water tables. Despite the high costs and depleting water tables, irrigated areas have increased steadily, making livelihoods even more precariously dependent upon sustainable groundwater management.

In recent years, global discussions on water scarcity have been dominated by considerable debate on the true value of water. This is because one of the reasons for misallocation, misuse and degradation of water is that is not priced to its true value (CVG 1997:13). There is general endorsement of the statement that water is a social, economic and environmental good because of the multiple roles it performs. But very little consensus exists on how it should be repeated in different contexts and what are its implications for governance and management of the resource, including inter-sectoral allocation, pricing and efficiency of use. This is particularly true for groundwater. Even in a market economy like the US, groundwater is usually considered as either an invaluable good or as a 'free' good (CVG 1997).

Nevertheless, worsening physical shortage of water on the one hand and scarcity of economically accessible water on the other, had preoccupied researchers with the fundamental question of the economic value of water, that is, whether water is being put to high-value use (Perry et al 1997) and the methodological questions involved in valuation (CVG 1997). Value of water is the price that users are willing to pay for use of the resource (MacGregor et al, 2000). Since water markets often do not exist for many uses and even when they exist are often imperfect, estimating the value of water is difficult. Economic value of a resource is the incremental economic output that could be realized through the use of the resource (Young 1996 cited in MacGregor 2000).

From the point of view of physical scarcity, north Gujarat is an 'absolute water scarce' region, where the per capital renewable water availability is only 427m^3/annum (IRMA/UNICEF 2001). With extremely limited surface water resources, groundwater is the major source of water for various uses throughout the year IRMA/UNICEF 2001; Kumar 2002). The fragile nature of water ecology in the region does not support water-intensive economic activities. But water use

(448m^3/annum) exceeds its renewable water resources, and 89.5 percent is used in farming, including dairying (IRMA/UNICEF 2001).

Groundwater mostly lies in the open access regime throughout India (Singh 1995) and so also in north Gujarat. Though groundwater is traded extensively for agriculture purpose in the region (Kumar and Singh 201), no price is to be paid for the use of water in aquifers. Besides this, well owners are not confronted with full marginal cost of abstraction due to a heavily subsidized flat rate system of electricity pricing in the farm sector (Kumar forthcoming). Therefore these markets are inefficient and imperfect and hence assessing the true economic value of the resource on the basis of prices is north appropriate.

The consequences of groundwater overdraft can be grave for north Gujarat in terms of its environment, the sustainability of agriculture, and the health of its people (Gass et al 1996). With groundwater degradation, the surface ecology, particularly biodiversity, soils and vegetative cover also undergo drastic, and often irreversible, degradation. With increasing level of fluoride in groundwater, which is the main source of the region's drinking water (IRMA/UNICEF 2001; Kumar 2002), public health costs of groundwater overdraft may become prohibitive too (Kumar 2002), public health costs of groundwater overdraft may become (Kumar 2002). The direct cost of depletion is also a topic of concern to farmers (Gass et al 1996; IRMA/UNICEF 2001), while the economic cost matters to the state government, which subsidises electricity in the farm sector.

Though the magnitude of depleting is high (the

average rate of decline of water levels ranging from 0.91m to 6.02m/annum in Mehsana (CGWB 1998), leading to scarcity (Kumar 2002; Shah et al 2003), and the price at which groundwater is traded is high (Dubash 2000; Kumar and Singh 2001; Mohanty and Ebrahim 1995) reflecting the scarcity value of the resource (Mohanty and Ebrahim 1995), the question often asked by policy-markers is whether the scarcity value is fully realized under existing uses, the most important being irrigation is that farmers and dairy production.

The underlying premise is that farmers who own tube wells enjoy unlimited access to the resource, are not fully confronted with the opportunity cost of using water due to heavily subsidized electricity, and divert water for growing crops that are economically inefficient. The other related research questions are negative consequences of groundwater depletion of the economics of farming significant; are the livelihood impacts of irrigation significant enough to continue subsidized electricity for groundwater pumping?

Knowing the total economic value of groundwater is important for determining the benefits of policies and actions aimed at addressing groundwater depletion problems (CVG 1997). This paper attempts to estimate the value derived from the use of groundwater in Banaskantha district of north Gujarat. The study had following objectives: *(1)* to analyse the livelihood impact of groundwater irrigation at the household level; *(2)* evaluate the economics of groundwater irrigation for typical farmer categories and analyse the economic consequences of resources of resource degradation; and *(3)* estimate the size of groundwater economy of the village.

The value of groundwater was assessment was assessed in terms of the size of the groundwater economy. In order to assess the size of the groundwater economy of the villages, the irrigated cropping pattern in the village, cattle size, and net incremental returns per unit area of irrigated crops and a livestock unit have been used as inputs.

Economic value of ground water (EVGW) was assessed by using the formula;

EVGW = (Total value product per unit irrigated area – [(PL*QL +) PF*QF) +(PIW)] *irrigated cropped area + (total value product per unit of cattle – CPCF*QCF)* No of cattle units.

Here, P stands for price and Q quantity. L, F and IW stand for labour, fertilizer and pesticides, and irrigation water. PIW is, therefore, the price of unit volume of irrigation water, but includes both depreciation for the capital investment and variable cost. QIE is the quantity of irrigation water per unit area.

Economics of groundwater irrigation was evaluated by comparing the gross economic returns from crop and milk production against their actual economic cost of production. The livelihood impact of groundwater irrigation was analysed by comparing the income from: *(a)* farming; *(b)* dairying; *(c)* farm-labour; and, *(d)* sale of water against the total annual family income. The detailed methodology and analytical procedure used in the study are given in Kumar et al (2004).

Structured questionnaires were administered to get details of various farm inputs and outputs and income from wage labour. Details of household in come of wage labour were obtained through a separate questionnaire. Semi-structured questionnaires were used to get insights into livelihood aspects of well irrigation, problems of groundwater over-exploitation; historical changes in well irrigation, and groundwater economy at he village level from groups of farmers and other stakeholder. Sometimes and open discussion with a group of farmers was conducted to get an overall idea about a particular village.

The study was restricted to four villages of Banaskantha district. It only focused on the private and economic costs and benefits of groundwater use, and did not consider the social and environmental costs and benefits. A sample of 30 farmers was covered including well owners, water buyers and partners in tube well companies from each of the four villages. The total sample size was 160, including 10wagelabourers from each village.

Cropping pattern: In the semi-arid Banaskantha district, in the absence of major surface irrigation schemes. Cropping is mainly governed by access to groundwater supplies. Tube wells operated by submersible pumps are the most common source of irrigation. Broadly, the district has three cropping seasons, winter (November to February), summer (March to June), and Kharif (July to October). Cropping system of the district comprises food crops, cash crops and fodder crops. Cropping pattern differs apropos the three seasons. It also varies across the region, the most important deciding factor being availability of groundwater.

Dairying is one of the primary occupations in this region [Kumar 2003]. All landowners keep some part of their land for producing fodder. Even the landless farmer's lease in small parcels to grow green fodder.

In winter, farmers go castor, wheat, mustard, barley, cumin, is baulk, rajgaro and fennel. In summer, they mostly grow pearl millet (bajra) andinkharif, cluster bean, sorghum (jowar), maize, green gram, seamen and groundnut.

Alfalfa and elephant grass are grown throughout the year to provide green fodder to the animals. The byproducts of the food crops wheat, pearl millet and sorghum form the major dry fodder for cattle, and the existing cropping pattern also reflects the needs for cattle, and the existing cropping pattern also reflects the needs of dairying, which is an integral part of the farming system. Also, cattle dung is used as manure for crop cultivation.

Some parts of the district have experienced a major shift in cropping pattern over time. The shift is from water-intensive crops to less water-intensive varieties. For example, till 1990, Khasa village was growing paddy and sugar cane as major crops, but there has since been complete shift to crops like sorghum, and castor. Area under food crops has remained more or less the same over a period of time. The cropping pattern shift has been characterized by a expansion in area under cash crops.

Cropping pattern of the four surveyed villages is given Table. In Khassa, castor is the major crop in the rabi season constitution around half of the total area (46.1 per cent). A similar trend is also found in Kumbhalmer (44.0 per cent) and Thanan (46.7 per cent). In Vansol, yam, castor and wheat are grown in almost equal proportions, at wheat (30.6 per cent), castor (33.66 6percent) and yam (22.7 per cent). During summer, mostly pearl millet is grown in all villages, and constitutes more than 60 per cent of the total cropping area. Maize is grown only in Thana as a kharif crop. In this season, cluster bean is the main crop in addition to sorghum. Winter and summer crops are fully irrigated, whereas in kharif, crops are given protective irrigation in case of monsoon failure.

Cattle Composition and Size: Dairying is the backbone of the rural economy in north Gujarat. The region has some of the biggest dairies is Asia. Dairying is also a highly water-intensive farming activity [Singh and Kishore 2003]. All villagers in this region have crossbred cows and Mehasani breed of buffaloes. This breed of animals has higher milk productivity than local breeds. Numbers of other animals such as bullocks, sheep and goats are negligible. Over the years, the buffalo population in the region has declined and that of crossbred cows has increased. In villages, cows are more in number than buffaloes. But the total number of buffaloes from all the four sample villages put together is 1.937; whereas the number of cows is only 924.

Though rearing a crossbred cow is more beneficial than rearing a buffalo, as found by Singh and Kishore (2003) in their recent study in Meshana, the cattle composition is dominated by buffaloes. If we divide the cattle composition into different stages of animal, like calving, pregnancy, lactating period and dry period, calving stage for a cow is 3.5 years and for buffalo it is 2.5 years. Lactation period for a cow is nine months and for buffalo it is 7-8 months. A buffalo gives milk 8.5 years of her life and a cow gives milk 9.5 years of life. After 10 years of its life a buffalo it is 7-8 months. A buffalo gives milk 8.5 years of her if and a cow gives milk 9.5 years of life. After 10 years of its life buffalo becomes dry; a cow becomes dry after 13years of its life. The composition of cattle at these different stages, in the sample of 100 families from four villages.

In the sample data of all the four villages, the proportion of milch cows is 47 per cent and that of milch buffalo is 45 %. Pregnant cows and buffaloes constitute 7 per cent each of the total number of cows and buffaloes. Proportion of dry buffalo to the total number of buffalo is 0.13 and that of dry cow is 0.06. In case of calf, it is 0.34 for cow and 0.39 of buffalo.

Privet costs and returns from groundwater irrigation: Since rain fall is concentrated in three-four months of monsoon season and in a few rainy days, irrigation is essential for winter and summer cropping. Cropping during these seasons is entirely dependent on well irrigation. Similarly, dairying is possible because of the irrigated green fodder and by-products of irrigated crops. Therefore, the entire income from irrigated crops and dairying is treated as the gross value product of well irrigation. But the deep groundwater table raises the cost of installation of well and water lifting. Fixed as well as variable costs were considered in estimating irrigation cost. The variable cost of irrigation was estimated using the figures of annul electricity charges paid by farmers and to total hours of irrigation. While estimating the cost of other inputs, the cost of contribution of family labour was not considered.

Results of the analyses of private cost and returns for Kumbhalme village are presented. The analysis shows that irrigation cost as a per cent age of the total input cost is quite significant for all the crops, and that it varies from village to village. It varies from 25 to 32 per cent for wheat, 30.2 per cent to 48.4 per cent to 49.9 per cent for summer jowar, and from 59.7 per cent to 69.4 percent for alfalfa. The irrigation cost is highest in the case of alfalfa, ranging from the lowest cost of RS. 18073 per ha in case of Vansol to Rs. 25,604 per ha in case of Kumbhalmer. The results for alfalfa were not estimated, as it is not commonly traded in the market. Almost every farmer in the study village produces it in his/he own farm. The estimates are based on the information of labourers and some landless farmers who purchase alfalfa.

There are significant variations in the most of irrigation and, consequently, net private returns for the same crop across villages. For instance, the net return from wheat varies from a low of Rs. 7,275 per ha to a high of Rs. 14, 545 per ha in case of Thana. The net returns for summer jowar varies from Rs. 349/ha to Rs. 6,362/ha. While pat of this could be attributed to yield differences, the most important factor is the cost of irrigation. The factors deciding cost of irrigation are capital investment in wells and pump sets, which is decided by the groundwater conditions; and variable cost of irrigation, which is decided by the installed pump capacity. They are largely governed by geo hydrological conditions, which vary across the region.

The private returns from dairying were estimated using average cost of cattle inputs and income gain from milk output per cattle unit. Here, the average figures for the entire cattle population available in the sample were taken. While estimating the cost of cattle rearing, the cost of all inputs such as green fodder, dry fodder, concentrate and water was worked out on the basis of their production cost, except for the concentrates. To calculate the cost of dry fodder, cost of production of the crop was divided between main product and by-product in the same proportion as that of the revenue generated from each. The net private returns from cattle rearing for all four villages are presented in Table 5. Net economic returns from copping and dairying. In input intensive irrigated agriculture, there are differences between the cost incurred by an individual and the costs incurred by society at large. For instance, in well irrigation, farmers are not confronted with the full cost of pumping groundwater due to the flat-rate mode of pricing electricity in the farm sector. Similarly, farmers are not confronted with the societal (social and environmental) cost of using water from aquifers, as they do not have to pay water taxes to cover these costs. Here we are analyzing the viability of irrigated production for society at large. However, only the direct economic costs and benefits are considered.

While analyzing viability, and environmental and social costs and benefits are not considered. To estimate the economics of groundwater irrigation, actual market prices of inputs wee used, rather than only private costs to the farmer. Irrigation is the most significant of all inputs in agriculture. Farmers in north Gujarat pay fixed electricity prices on the basis of pump capacity, at subsidized rates. Also, while estimating economic costs, opportunity cost of engaging family labour was considered. Farmers have to obtain the rest of the inputs of cultivation at the market price.

Part of the analysis included estimation of the difference between actual cost of electricity generation and distribution to the farmer. It was found that farmers actually incur just half of the actual economic cost in terms of irrigation cost. The economic cost per hour of irrigation varies from Rs 64.1 for Khasa to Rs. 21.2 for Vansol, whereas the private cost of irrigation per hour varies from Rs 30.7 for Kumbhalmer to Rs 9.8 for Thana.

Cattle rearing farmers usually do not purchase fodder from the market. Farmers who do not own sufficient land generally get land on lease to produce green fodder, or work as agricultural labour to get on-third of the produce. While evaluating the economics of well irrigation, cost and benefits of main products of crops have been considered. Since all by-products are used as inputs in cattle rearing, the net output from dairying is also considered in the economics of well irrigation. The figures of net income from dairying per cattle unit are separately given.

It shows that the net economic returns are negative for some irrigated crops, but positive for milk production. Part of the reason is that in dairying, the allocated cost of production of crop by-products is used in estimating input costs, whereas in case of conventional crops, the full economic cost of production and market price of inputs are used. Groundwater irrigation leads to positive economic benefits when both crops and dairying become part of an integrated farming system. Dairying becomes a high-valued used for the by-products of farming, which otherwise do not fetch high market price.

Size of groundwater economy of the study villages; size of groundwater economy is estimated on the basis of : *(1)* net private returns from crops grown and dairy farming in the study villages estimated through primary surveys; and *(2)* secondary data on irrigated cropping pattern and cattle population. Net returns per hectare of each crop to an individual farmer were first estimate. In case of farm outputs that are used as cattle inputs, the actual cost of production was estimated and deducted form the gross income form cattle rearing, a part from other cattle inputs, to arrive at the newt income per unit of cattle.

The total incremental value of agricultural outputs generated through well irrigation was estimated to be Rs. 3.24 crore. It shows that dairying accounts for a major share of the groundwater economy in all the villages. The share a of dairying in the overall size of the farm economy varies from 44.8 % in the case to Thana to 75.3 % in the case of Vansol, whereas contribution of crops such as wheat, pearl millet and jowar is less than 10 %. However, dairying becomes profitable only because of the cheap inputs available to dairy farmers, especially dry fodder, in the form of by-products of wheat, peal millet and jowa grown. One the other hand, if they decide to go for purchase cost of production could rise too high to make milk production an unattractive proposition. In fact, in cases where groundwater capacity hits a large number of farmers, dairying is continued with purchased dry and green fodder from neighbouring villages as a short-term strategy for sustaining livelihoods.

Nevertheless, if the farmers grow only conventional crops and do not keep cattle, the income realized from sale of crop by-products would be too insignificant to make irrigated farming viable. Dairying helps in value addition. Therefore, it is difficult to judge, on the basis of the results of the analysis presented here, which activity is more profitable. There is a need to recognize the integrated nature of farming system with right size of the groundwater economy across the sample villages owing to variations in cost of irrigation and irrigated area, and the size of cattle population.

Livelihood Impacts of Well Irrigation: It has been demonstrated that the rural economy of Banaskantha, which lacks major manufacturing units, is controlled by access to well irrigation, without which crop cultivation and dairying are practically impossible. Access to well irrigation enables rural households to engage in agricultural operations throughout the year and enhance the returns from land. In the study area, due to tube well irrigation, which ensures reliable water supply throughout the yea, productivity of land is quite remarkable. Well-owning farmers normally take to crops; and sometimes a third crop as well, thereby maximizing the gross returns from farms. Well irrigation also negates family labour in farming operations, thee by generating employment of the surplus, unskilled labour force. Since labour, which forms a significant chunk of input costs is domestic; the net income from irrigated agriculture is high.

Irrigation also increases the availability of green and dry fodder through out the year, which enables farmers to keep high-yielding varieties of buffaloes and crossbred cows, in an otherwise biomass-scarce region. Availability of dry and green fodder from owns farms reduce the cost of milk production. Family labour is employed in dairying, which is labour-intensive; women engage in fodder cutting and grass collection, while men are engaged in feeding and milking the animals. On the other hand, farmers who do not own wells get water from well owners of a crop-sharing basis and are able to cultivate even during non-monsoon seasons. For the landless, who is unskilled well irrigation provides round-their-year employment within their village. However the size of farm employment opportunities depends very much on the landholding pattern and the size of irrigated product in the villages.

In a nutshell, it can be said the agriculture becomes a primary occupation and a major source of livelihood for farm households in rural areas, it access to well irrigation is ensured. The food security situation has improved as a wide variety of cereals and pulses, vegetables and milk produced the farms are used for domestic consumption. The over all purchasing power of the family has improved. It can be said that groundwater has played a significant role in stabilising the livelihood of all section of people, well-owners, and water purchaser sand wage labourers. But the extent of livelihood contribution of well irrigation also depends on the income contribution from well irrigation for irrigators and farm labour generated for labourers, and the presence or absence of other sources of livelihood.

The livelihood impact of well irrigation was analysed for well owners, water purchasers and agricultural labourers. To estimate income from well irrigation, we have included incomes from agricultural produce, dairying, wage labour and income from water sales, if any.

It shows the proportion of income generated from irrigated agriculture the income generated from all sources. It is also evident that well irrigation is contribution nearly three-fourth to the total income. Contribution of well irrigation to over all livelihoods is more in case of water buyers than well owners. In case of wage labourers, the proportion varies from village to village. As the area under well irrigation is limited, the labourers have to depend on some non-farm sources such as diamond cutting and driving. The cultivators have taken to overall livelihood is more in case of water buyers than well owners. In case of wage labourers, the proportion varies from village to village. As the area under well irrigation is limited, the labourers have to depend on some non-farm sources such as diamond cutting and driving. The cultivators have taken to dairying as a source of livelihood as they find crop cultivation increasingly becoming unviable. Dairying, the mainstay of the household economy, is also influenced by well irrigation. The higher the amount of water available, the more livestock they maintain.

The contribution of irrigated agriculture to livelihood security is significant. This is in spite of the fact that overall rise in cost of irrigation forces small farmers to go for wage labour. In some area where well have dried up, people chooses to migrate to the nearby towns and cities. If this condition persists, it could threaten the sustainability of communities living in these rural areas. Historical changes in economics of well irrigation: Economics of well irrigation can be conditioned by adjusting he cropping system [Llamas 2002]. But for a given cropping system, the economic dynamic of well irrigation is decided by the capital cost of the irrigation system, variable costs of irrigation including the energy cost and maintenance costs, and gross area commanded by the well. Geo-hydrology is an important factor, which has a high bearing on these variables [Kumar et al 2001].

Analysis of historical changes in the dynamic of well irrigation was based on primary data collected form the survey through call method. Based on data collected from farmers vis-à-vis the condition of the water table, wells, pump sets and well command, the present cost of well irrigation was estimated for selected crops, and compared with that of the past. Irrigation cost was taken on the constant price, taking year 2000 bas base year and 6 per cent as rate of inflation for all the years. The analysis shows that cost of irrigation per hectare of cropped are has gone up across villages for all the crops studied, though notable differences in percentage rise were observed between villages. For instance, the cost of irrigation of wheat increased form Rs. 1960/ha to Rs. 4595/ha in Thana. Similarly, the cost of irrigation of mustard went up form Rs. 1482/ha to Rs. 2952/ha in Kumbhalmer during 1970-2003.

In thana, the water table has dropped by nearly 60 feet in the past decade. With the water table touching 180 feet, open wells have gone dry. Now only rich farmers who can afford high pump capacity tube wells are able to do irrigated farming. The cost of irrigation has resulted insignificant change in the cost of well irrigation. However, on a time scale, the area under irrigation for each crop and gone up remarkable for the sample farmers. For instance, area under wheat has shown a growth of 15 per cent. The area under cash crops has also increased much more than the growth in area under food crops. Hence it should be inferred that farmers are able to offset the income losses due to increased irrigation through expansion in are under irrigation, which is enabled by the advantage of deep pumping technology.

Private returns from crops irrigated by groundwater, including dairying, are positive and remarkable. This is in spite of the fact that irrigation forms a major chunk of the input costs in farming, ranging from 25 per cent for wheat in Khasa to 70 per cent for alfalfa in Kumbhalmer. Groundwater irrigation is vital for sustaining dairy production, which extensively uses the by-products of farm produce as cattle in puts. The net returns from milk production are also quite significant.

The net economic returns are negative for some irrigated crops, but positive for milk production. Groundwater irrigation leads to positive economic benefits when both crops and dairying become part of an integrated farming system.

The economic value of groundwater, estimated as the incremental value of the from output generated form groundwater use in the four study villages, is Rs 3.24 crore annually. A major share of the net economic output generated by irrigated agricultural is form milk production.

Groundwater plays a vital role in improving the livelihood of those who have taken up farm-based occupations. Groundwater irrigation is a major source of livelihood not only for well owners, but also for water buyers and farm labourers.

Over exploitation and consequent depletion of groundwater has led to a sharp rise n the cost of well irrigation, but farmers are able to offset the income losses through expansion in area under irrigation, which is enabled a by technology shift from dug-well irrigation to tube well irrigation.

To conclude, in the area under investigation, agriculture and dairying are highly dependent on availability of and access to groundwater. The private returns form well irrigation is significant in all the study villages. The economic value of groundwater use in agriculture expressed as the size of groundwater economy of the villages, and estimated as the net value product generated from groundwater irrigation in these villages, is quite high. Te lion's share of the net farm output generated through groundwater use in agriculture comes from dairying. Groundwater irrigation also contributes significantly to improving the livelihood of the landless as well as farming households. However, depletion of groundwater and changes in water table conditions have led to a sharp increase in the cost of irrigation, resulting in reduced economic returns from farming. Farmers are able to sustain irrigated production because of the subsidized electricity available in the farm sector.

The fact that the extent of groundwater depletion is significant enough to affect income from irrigated agriculture, and that livelihood contribution of groundwater is still significant and widespread, demands greater societal concern and public investment to ensure sustainable groundwater use in agriculture instead of pumping regulation/legislation to ban pumping. One of the ways to achieve this will be large-scale-recharge intervention like the Sujalam Sufalam scheme, recently launched by the Gujarat government to improve groundwater condition in the region. A critical water management intervention to address the issues of sustainable groundwater use is demand management in agriculture. Pricing of electricity used for groundwater Pumping is an important tool for demand management.

Two previous studies from the region had shown that economics of irrigated farming is more elastic to quality of power supply than the price of electricity used for pumping groundwater is an important tool for demand management.

Two previous studies from the region had shown that economics of irrigated farming is more elastic to quality of power supply than the price of electricity used for pumping groundwater [kumar and Singh 2001], and the tariff levels at which demand for electricity and water become elastic to pricing changes do not affect the returns form irrigated agriculture and hence are variable for a socio-economic point of view as farmers use water more efficiently and also shift to water-efficient crops at higher electricity tariffs [Kumar forthcoming]. Use of micro-irrigation technologies would also contribute to making groundwater use in agriculture more efficient and sustainable. Policies designed to promote micro-irrigation systems should integrate concerns such as livelihood contribution of groundwater irrigation and the criticality of dairying in the overall frame economy, especially of poor small and marginal farmers, who have to purchase water from well owners. This means it would be particularly important of poor small and marginal farmers to existing crops as they will not have the option of shifting to water-efficient crops that often involve high risks and long duration for cash returns

8

Significance of Sardar Sarovar Project

Few large irrigation projects in India have been as elaborately planned as the Sardar Sarovar Project (SSP), incorporating as it did the lessons of decades of irrigation project design and management with water user associations building their own distribution systems. However, as it unfolds, the institutional reality of the project is vastly different form its plans. If SSP is to chart a different course form scores of earlier large irrigation projects, it must invent and put into place new less cores of earlier large irrigation projects, it must invent and put into place new rules of the irrigation management game.

Thirty years in planning, over 15 years in construction and some Rs. 15,000 crore of investment later, the Sardar Sarovar Project's vision is now ready to unfold. When fully commissioned, the project will use 5,600 km of main and branch canals and 66,000 km of distribution network (including distributaries and minors) to deliver 9.8 km of irrigation water to 1.8 million ha of land. Besides, the SSP is also expected to make a major dent in the rural and urban drinking water needs of the state and to help recharge groundwater aquifers in intensively groundwater-irrigated area of north Gujarat and Saurashtra. If all these targets are fully or even substantially met, the SSP will indeed prove to be the lifeline of Gujarat. And this will happen if its optional strategy, that is, key assumptions made during the planning phase about its manner of operation hold. The SSP's operational strategy was put to test in rabi 2002, and its key elements are:

The project will create distribution infrastructure such that each village has one or more pucca minors depending upon its cultivable command area (CCA); a distribution system below the minor including lined sub-minors delivering water to 40-60 ha checks, and field channels further down to serve 5-8 ha sub checks, will be created by the irrigation community. The thinking presumably was that by involving the irrigation community in the design and creation of the distribution infrastructure below the minor, the project would not only invite genuine partnership with the community but also provide an organizing logic for the "water user association (WUA)".

The irrigation community in each minor (Serving a village service area) will form a WUA whose responsibility will be to: *(a)* mobilize community labour and resources to create the water distribution system blow the minor; *(b)* arrange orderly distribution of irrigation water within the command; *(c)* ensure future maintenance and upkeep of the distribution system below the minor while the canal infrastructure up to the minor level is maintained and operated by the SSP; *(d)* collect water fee at the rate of Rs. 157/ irrigation/ha, of which Rs 7 would go back to the WUA as a subsidy to meet administrative expenses. The idea was that participatory irrigation management (PM) in the SSP should start at the beginning. Rather then come midstream when system managers have taken all crucial design decisions.

The project will provide will provide only 3\21" delta of water in five irrigations during the rabi season; no summer irrigation was envisaged, nor was it envisaged that Narmada water would be used to raise perennial, water-intensive crops like sugar cane and banana. SSP planners' idea was to cover large areas through extensive irrigated command. The logic of rationing water was to stem, at the outset, the propensity of early command areas at the head of the system forming the habit of water-intensive agriculture.

The SSP's primary responsibility was to be upkeep of the infrastructure up to the minor level, and timely delivery of water on volumetric basis to each village service area of the WUA, which would collect and aggregate indents from individual farmers in the command. That done, it was expected that the WUAs would take over the responsibility of water distribution with the village service area. SSP would not consider water distribution with the village service area. SSP would not consider water indents by individual farmers unless these were routed through the WUA. This was expected to result in the division of operation and maintenance (O and M) responsibility and costs in which the project was to take the responsibility of those part of O and M that require technical and engineering competence of a high order, while WUAs wee to operate and maintain local infrastructure within the village service areas where the knowledge of local conditions is critical.

The system is planned for sophisticated, computerized water control from control rooms strewn along branches and distributaries throughout the command; while the control rooms are ready, thee water control infrastructure will take a long time to install and commission. As a result, for several years, volumetric water control will be operated manually, if at all. The basic idea is to introduce volumetric delivery and charge at all levels right from the beginning.

As visions and strategies go, the early years of the operation of the SSP will be critical; they will decide whether the project will run by the original vision outlined above, or by a new evolutionary operational framework even superior to the original vision, or regress into an operational mode in which the SSP will follow in the footsteps of other major irrigation projects, where achievements on all counts have fallen far short of expectations.

The SSP is now poised at that crucial juncture. The SSP too is getting ready to be 'run in' like a new engine. Starting in rabi 2002, SSP has begun to release irrigation to some 80,000 ha of its command in Narmada,m, Bharuch and Vadodara districts where canal and distribution infrastructure up to the minor level is fully or partially ready. While the full reservoir capacity is likely to be created one the dam height is raised to 135 m, it will take 10-15 years before the canal network gets constructed to cover the entire command area of the project. Until then, the SSP will gradually evolve, adding new areas in its irrigated command every year. In this process of evolution, the experience of these formative years will prove decisive in three ways: *(a)* System manger as well as users' behaviour and practices in the first years will take the shape of habits, which will be difficult and painful to change later. *(b)* The behaviour, practices and habits allowed to form in early parts of the command will define the norms, rules behaviour and habits in the new areas being brought under the command as the project evolves. *(c)* Early years will decide whether the actual operational framework of the project is faithful to the original vision or where it is superior, comparable or inferior to it.

The SSDP field staff has already done some amount of WUA organizing work in the 800 villages encompassing the first year command of 80,000 ha.. Typically, a group of 11 leading, forward looking farmers, generally representing all or most of the chalks constituting the command area in each minor (sometimes, more than one minor) comprise the management committee of the WUA and also act as promoter, with one of the members nominated as (often cajoled to become) the president. Over 800 UWUAs have been registered as cooperatives under the Cooperative Act. However, registering WUAs as cooperatives is quite different from catalyzing functional WUAs that begin to undertake all the tasks they are expected to perform. The critical challenge facing the SSP is to activate and energies the 800-odd minor level WUAs so that they begin to play the role envisaged for them by the SSP vision.

During late 2002; IWMI-Tata researchers worked together with the field staff and engineers of the SSP to develop a first-hand assessment of the preparedness of irrigation communities to receive and utilize Narmada water for irrigation. Some 40 villages in different pats of the command were covered. Subsequently, the IWMI-Tata programme; continued with field surveys and studies in these villages. The objectives of this field research were:

To develop a quick situation analysis of the conditions in each village covered, including the size of farm lands, number of irrigators, socio-economic structure, copping pattern, existing irrigation sources, farm productivity, and such other.

To assess the preparedness of the irrigation groups to receive Narmada waters and arrange for their orderly distribution.

To assess the level of user comfort with the SSP water pricing (which is higher compared to government water pricing in all other surface irrigation system) and the mode of collection of water fees and its reimbursement to SSP.

To understand the general state of the WUA, its internal dynamic, public awareness about its existence, functions and future role; and

To develop an assessment of the likelihood of the SSP vision, outlined earlier, playing out in reality; and to develop a prognosis of what might happen if it does not.

The general situation in the 40 villages covered by fieldwork was highly variable. Some villages near Kevadia Colony, near the head of the system, have had a small area irrigated by Narmada water on a trial basis; some more area in Bharuch district too received some surface irrigation from small and medium irrigation projects, such as the Deo project. Barring these small patches, the entire area commanded in this first phase has never seen canal irrigation before. However, we found that even villages which had some canal irrigation experience had no experience of farmer management of water distribution. In Devalia and Madhodar minors, where the sub-minors too were constructed by the SSP Nigam under a pilot, WUAs were formed some three years back and were supposed to manage water distribution and water fee collection. However, in reality, the water rotation and water fee collection. However, in reality, the water distribution and water fee collection. However, in reality, the water rotation roster is given to them by the Nigam officials and the WUA has done little of its won rule-marking work. Moreover, where as in Mahi and Ukai-Kakrapar commands, we found vibrant farmer organizations like dairy and sugar cooperatives, the villages we visited in the SSP command had virtually no experience in successful farmer organizations at the local level. If anything people had bitter memories of all manners of cooperatives that have either swindled them or become defunct.

Groundwater irrigation was fairly well developed in some parts but absent in there such as in Bharuch. Tank irrigation – by gravity flow and through life irrigation with diesel pumps and rubber pipes— however was found to be common. Near Jambusar, where large tracts suffer from primary salinity, agriculture has been underdeveloped and careful application of surface irrigation can boost the economy. Unlike the command areas of Ukai-Kakarapar, Mahi and other canal systems, were patidaars dominate te farming population, in the 40 villages we visied, kshartriya dominate the farming, and they are not as well known as the patidaars for their agrarian entrepreneurship. While we found stray cases of Saurashtra Patels having acquired land and settled in the command area, there seemed no evidence of large-scale strategic land acquisition by enterprising farmers from outside the command yet. In general, we found kshatriyas (Jadejas, Darbars, etc), Parmars, Prajapatis and a spattering of Harijans and tribal in most of the villages. Some of the villages in Bharuch district have mixed Hindu and Muslim populations. Compared to the Mahi command area in Kheda district, for instance, the villages we visited were agriculturally far more backward; and the onset of irrigation will no doubt perk up the rural economy of this region in three to five years. Our surmise was that each of the 80,000 ha would produce at least Rs. 8-10000 per ha in incremental value added thanks to the Narmada (direct irrigation plus more productive well irrigation): and the cost of Narmada irrigation will be less than 10 per cent of this increased value added from farm land.

All the villages visited had taken some action to form WUAs under prompting form SSP field staff. However, almost everywhere, water we found was only management committees (MCs) with a president-designate. A few MCs had already had a general body meeting, but none had actually begun enrolling irrigators as formal members of WUAs. A subsequent IWMI-Tata study [Talati and Liebrand 2003] sowed tat less than 3 per cent of the farmers benefiting from Narmada water had paid their WUA membership fees. The study, which surveyed farmers in 12 villages of SSP command, also found that while most farmers know the members of the management committee, 62.5

per cent did not know the purpose of forming WUA; 50 per cent did not know about the meeting in which WUA was formed; 82 per cent know no the in about the byelaws of the WUA and none know about the rules and regulations of the WUA. Expectedly, no WUA performed any of the three essential tasks hey are expected to perform, viz. indent collation and water allocation, orderly distribution of water and collection of water charge.

SSP's pricing and other policies too have been evolving only recently; and they had not yet been fully communicated to all the MCs. There was also some confusion amongst MCs about the by-laws and specific clauses contained in them. Within SSP staff too, there was lack of clarity about how the report of the government of Gujarat's task force on PIM would affect the SSP WUAs. All in all, at the time of our field wok, there were great confusion and ambiguity about the design of WUAs, the by-laws the specific role of WUAs, and the SSP. Later field studies suggest that there is no major improvement in this condition since then.

We had expected to find some work initiated by irrigation communities at the village level to create the water distribution system below the minor. However, in none of the 40 villages was there any move in this direction. In fact, we found significant resistance to the idea; in many villages, MC members categorically told us that sub-minors and field channels would never get built unless the government does it. There was some ambiguity about what the government/ SSP will do to help; engineers accompanying us told MCs that the government had recently taken the decision to acquire land for building sub-minors. Some

MCs felt tat this would be welcome. The general impression field staff gave farmer was that sub-minors to the chalk level must be pucca-lined; and farmers seemed daunted by its cost.

In any case, form our interaction with 40 village communities; we understood that it is very unlikely that rigatoni communities will construct sub-minor and field channels in a hurry, if at all. Half-hearted statements and rumors that government might after all take over the responsibility of building distribution systems within village service areas has further educed the chances that irrigation communities would take any initiative in this direction [Thomass 2004]. A detailed case study of social dynamics in two chaks of the SSP command suggested that farmers do engage in primitive forms of fragmented collective action in building water courses within small proportions of the chaks but that conflicts amongst sub-grounds hinder or frustrate sub efforts. It also does not help at this informal fragmented private and collective action results in the design of water courses that is very different from the standardized design evolved by the SSP planners, who are therefore not sympathetic to such un-coordinated attempts by groups of irrigators trying to secure access to Narmada irrigation [Thomas 2004]. But the SSP designed distribution systems are unlikely to get implemented for a long time to come, if ever.

What seems far more likely is that tiny areas adjoining the minors will be flow-irrigated, but a lot more area will be irrigated by lifting water from canals through diesel pumps and rubber pipes. Even farmers who can irrigate by gravity flow often prefer lifting water and conveying it through rubber pipes to avoid conflict with upstream farmers and to better control the flow (Thomas 2004). This mode of irrigation from canals, drains and tanks is already quite popular in many parts. Almost every village we visited had 10-20 diesels pump renters who also provide up to 1,000-1,500 feet of rubber pipes. Conveying lifted water 1-1.5 km using rubber pipes is quite common in the area. Therefore, rather than investing money and labour in building field channels and sub-minors, farmers will very likely us lift irrigation on a large scale. In many villages we covered, we found that farmers were already preparing to invest in diesel pump sets and pipes. Once they see water in the minors, it is quite likely 5-10,000 new diesel pumps and some 4-5,000 km of flexible pipes will come into the command area. The going rental rate for 5-7.5 hp diesel pumps was Rs 50-60/hour but with the growing density of pumps, these rates will fall. In any case, pump irrigation markets will be a huge presence in the 80,000 ha command.

This was confirmed by a study we carried out during November 2002-March 2003. The Talai-Liebrand (2003) survey of 543 irrigation in 12 villages of the SSP command during rabi 2002-03 showed that of the 1,150 ha irrigated with Namada water in the 12 villages surveyed, 727 ha were irrigated by lifting water, and the remained by gravity flow or by the use of siphons. It also showed that for every rupee they paid to the SSP Nigam for water charges, irrigators spent Rs. 2.25 on lifting I from minors. Pump irrigation markets were booming with farmers lifting and transporting water up to 2,500 feet. Farmers in 10 of the 12 villages surveyed invested in 40 diesel pump sets with 5 to 8 hp capacity and 14,024 meters delivery pipes—of various makes and materials such as rubber, HDPE, fertilizer bags and PVC—to operate on the newly catalysed water markets. A pump dealer interviewed by Talati and Liebrand was upbeat about business: he had already sold 30 pump sets in rabi 2002-03 itself, and expected to sell 350 the following year.

Providing SSP's water allocation of 5,200 m^3/ha will require an average of 150-200 hours of pump irrigation. At 150 hours/ha, the total value of water lifted to irrigate 80,000 ha will be around Rs. 60 crore. In some villages, farmers did complain tat compared to other government sources, SSP is proposing a higher water fee. The government also intends to levy the same fee for lift irrigation while the normal policy is to charge half-rate for lift irrigation from canals and tanks. But our overall impression was that farmers will easily accept the higher water fees proposed. The SSP official water rate at Rs. 150/ha for five irrigations for 80,000 ha should be just Rs 6 crore, around 10 percent of the value they place on water. Thus, the SSP water fees are just a small fraction of the actual value farmers place on that water, and should be not difficult to collect at all; this however downs not mean that SSP will be able to collect its Rs. 6 crore/season easily.

Some aspects we found in our interactions with farming groups which may have serious implications for the way the situation will evolve, have to do with farmers' perceptions about SSP as an organization:

(a) While farmers elevated with the real prospects of getting Narmada water, they were also angered by repeated un kept promises from SSP about when water would be available; farmers we met understood the constraints the project faced but felt that what SSP and its field staff say cannot be relied upon.

(b) This was further complicated by the fact that different members of the field staff gave different messages to the irrigation communities. In one village, for instance, the staff accompanying us explained that WUAs would have to collect water fees from flow irrigators as well as lift irrigators at the same rate. In the same village, another group of SSP staff had told farmers that same morning that the government's problem was of maximizing the use of water so farmers can pump at would without worrying about water charges. Such conflicting messages from SSP staff resulted in the erosion of the credibility of the organization amongst farmers; this can only be resolved by having a clear and aggressive communication strategy for SSP.

(c) Often in good faith and almost causally, SSP field staff liberally made commitments to irrigation communities to fix their specific local problems. In some villages, farmers came with complaints that some of their lands were waterlogged; in one village, the community wanted the bed of the minor raised so they could use siphons; in several, they wanted the SSP Nigam to provide water to fill their tanks; and in others, where the paddy crop was burning because of moisture stress, farmers wanted Narmada water released immediately to save the paddy crop. Field staff accompanying us agreed so solve all their problems or at least to took into them. However, irrigators as well as SSP staff were certain that most of these commitments would not be kept, often because it is very difficult, or even impossible, to solve each individual farmer's problem in such a larger system. Yet, farmers will not forget these commitments and will use them as a stick to beat the SSPs with.

(d) One idea that was deeply ingrained in the minds of farmers is that SSP's need to release water into the system is greater and stronger than the farmer's need to use the water; allowing this impression to continue must further erode SSP's capability to establish an orderly institutional arrangement for irrigation.

(e) Similarly, farmers and management committees we met assigned no seriousness o urgency to SSP's insistence on the operating practices it intends to purse. For example, most farmers did not believe that water indents will not be honored unless they are made through WUAs; that WUAs do not make an indent will not get water; that WUAs which do not pay their dues will be refused water for the next irrigation; and that lift irrigation will actually be charged at the same rate as flow irrigation. It seemed to us that farmers take the SSP and the government so lightly that they wee totally nonchalant about SSP's new water policy, which they did not believe would be vigorously implemented.

Overall, based on a brief stint of field work during 2003 and follow up studies later, our assessment is that it is unlikely that the overall vision of the SSP for irrigation management will play out for several seasons to come. Farmers are certainly not ready but we think that even the SSP is not quite ready to implement its strategy. For example, neither farmers nor field staff knows even now where to obtain forms for indenting water. Field staff have not thought about what course of action is to be adopted in village which have minors but have not submitted their water dints, or if farmers begin to lift water en masse without submitting the indent.

It is unlikely that even in the long run, irrigation communities and WUAs will build below-the –minor distribution system of the kind that SSP expects them to build. Most villages will prefer instead to use lift irrigation and rubber pipes to distribute water. This means that there will be no planned, orderly water distribution by the WUAs. Instead, pump irrigation markets will proliferate. From the viewpoint of water us efficiency as also of economical use of water, this arrangement would in some ways be even superior than the sub-minors and field channels envisaged by the SSP. Pipes will minimizes seepage; and farmers paying Rs. 50-60/hour of lift irrigation will strive to minimise wasteful use of water. There, in our judgment markets may not be necessarily bad and may even result in better use of the 21″ delta that SSP plans to provide.

Two issues which are bothersome about this are: use of energy and equitable distribution of water. Pump irrigation based distribution will mean avoidable use of 150-200 litres of fuel/ha; and it will be useful to examine if improved water use efficiency justifies this substantial incremental cost. A detailed and proper analysis of private, community and social cost benefit issues involved in choosing between lift-based and gravity based distribution systems is strongly indicated.

They key gain from the former is that it will not require setting aside farm land for sub minors and field channels, which may cost Rs. 4-5 lakh per minor, especially if land is acquired after irrigation arrives, as will be the case in these parts of the Narmada command. SSP has already been estimating the cost of a fairly good distribution system at around around Rs. 10-12.5 lakh/village; and a good part of it will require regular, annual maintenance. Contrast this with 507.5 hp pumps and 50 km of flexi pipes, with a total capital investment of around Rs. 10-12.5 lakh, to distribute water over 500 ha. The annual fuel cost at 150 litres/ha would be Rs. 15,000. So in opting for lift based pump irrigation markets over organising for the construction of gravity flow distribution systems, a village irrigation community is paying around is 15 lakh/year (plus the annual wear and tear, and replacement costs of pumps and pipes) to save two costs: *(a)* farm land, labour and other material need to build channels; and *(b)* transaction cost of organizing to build a common property distribution system.

Gravity irrigation systems have their own equity issues between head-tail reach farmers. In a lift irrigation based water distribution system that may soon domine SSP command, equity issues will take a different spin in which topography will play an important part. Depending upon the location of their farms in relation to the minor, and the topography of the area, different farmers will have differential access the canal irrigation. Lands adjoining the minor will get plentiful gravity flow; their owners will be the most privileged class. Owners of hands, which can get canal water by using siphons, will also be privileged because they will not have to spend on lifting. Owners of fields further away and/or higher than the minor will be forced to lift; and those who are too resource poor to own their own pumps and pipes will spend the most for irrigation. Since the lift involved is low, perhaps it would be useful to promote low lift diesel and even manual and bullock operated pumps for water distribution.

What might be the role of WUAs and PIM in the Narmada context, if distribution of water below the minor will be done by private lift irrigation suppliers? Considerably more limited, in our view, than would be the case under gravity flow distribution. Indeed, the principal role the WUA would now be expected to play is of collecting water fees from irrigators and indenting water on their behalf from SSP.

In the immediate future, SSP can do little either to strengthen WUAs by capacity building work or to encourage irrigation communities to build distribution infrastructure since there is no time left. Over a medium to long run, however, it should keep making efforts to do both. What it can do now, however, is important and can profoundly affect the way the project's O and M evolve over the coming years. Some of these are listed below;

Indents for Irrigation Water: The best and quickest way of energising WUAs into functional bodies is for SSP o ensue that water indents are accepted only through WUA; and that no farmer who has not submitted an indent through the WUS is allowed to use irrigation from the minor, either by gravity or lit. In order that this happens, prior to each irrigation season, SSP needs to move fast, make indent forms available to WUA MCs and get them to complete these forms and submit them in a campaign mode. Advance collection of water fees: This can be another measure that will energies WUAs. Although theme is a widely used practice in Gujarat and elsewhere to collect irrigation fees after irrigation is over, we believe that this is the prime reason behind the low collection ratio. SSP's current policy offers WUAs 10 percent discount for advance payment. However, in our view, this gives irrigation communities scope to avoid having to organize now; MCs will take a laid back attitude because they can wait until after the season is over to approach members for dues. This opportunity should not be given. Instead SSP should ask all those WUAs who want irrigation water in rabi 2002 to pay their water fees in advance. Doing this will mean that MCs will have to call the general body meeting, and ask irrigators to pay up the water fees, which is the first step in catalyzing effective WUAs.

Announce an irrigation schedule and adhere to it strictly and at all costs: At present there is so much uncertainty and fluidity in the thinking of farmers and the SSP field staff that nobody can say for sure when will the fist irrigation be released, and how water will move around the system. Under this situation, WUAs would find it difficult to even their indents. The SSP should finalise an irrigation schedule as soon as possible and widely disseminate it. It should clearly state which minors will be un at full supply during which weeks, the total number of weeks that water will be provided and so on, so that farmers can plan their cropping patterns and schedules. Once these schedules are announced, they should be adhered to strictly. Doing this will enable MCs to call general body meeting and stat collecting advance water fees.

Establish Rules of the Game: The key task to be performed at this stage is to establish the rules of the game by which SSP will operate. Farmers now look at SSP as 'sarka mai-baap'. SSP needs to break out of this mould and establish a fair business relationship with users. This requires that its organization treats farmers as customers, like all good businesses and utilities do; at the same time, it needs to ensure that basic rules of the business are adhered to by both the parties. So SSP should provide a specified quantity of water along a specified schedule to irrigation communities that have indented water and paid for it in advance. Those that have not indented or not paid must be prevented from using Narmada water, no matter what. If this rule is not enforced in the first year, chances are that it will never be.

Mechanisms for Rule Enforcement: This is easier said than done. If minors in a certain distributaries are running at full capacity for seven days, how do WUA's catch defaulting farmers who lift water? How does SSP field staff ensure that WUAs, which have not filed there indent or paid their advance do not encourage their farmers to lift water straight from the distributaries or breach a nearby minor? Enforcing these rules will be the biggest challenge for SSP. Catching all cases of unauthorized use will be impossible; but a functional level of rule compliance can and must be achieved. If SSP meets this challenge well in the first years, by catching a significant proportion of cases of unauthorized irrigation and meting out exemplary penalty, rule-violation will decline in the future. But if numerous cases of unauthorized irrigation remain undetected and unchecked, anarchy will prevail, and it will become progressively more difficult to check it in the future.

The chaos currently prevailing in the SSP command is symptomatic of most canal irrigation projects In India. Although researchers still hark back to the philosophy of command area development (CAD) programs (Upadhyaya 2004), it is by now evident that these have done little to improve and sustain the performance of surface irrigation projects. Recent studies of major, medium and minor irrigation projects in six Indian state placed into bold relief how irrigation commands of all surface irrigation systems shrinking (Joy and Paranjape 2003, Meher 2003, Rajagopal 2003, shah 2003, Patil and Doraiswamy 2003, Vashinshtha et al 2003). These underscore the fact that while we have learnt to design and build irrigation systems, we have a long way to go in managing them to achieve their full potential for sustainable performance. Canal irrigation in India is at crossroads; and as a new large project, SSP can offer institutional answers with implications far beyond its own command area.

A default option for SSP is tighten Administration within its existing operating framework by gearing up the SSP and government machinery to ensure tight rule enforcement. But the logistics of doing this present a frightening prospect. It would imply intensive, round the clock campaigns to minor water use at all levels of the system. Based on our assessment of how far SSNL is willing to go—and how long it can sustain that way rule enforcement in this situation requires a level of effort that is unlikely in the governmental mode on a sustainable basis.

An alternative is to explore the Chinese approach to energies its local bureaucracy by restructuring its incentives. Facing much the same problems as Indian irrigation management has faced, the Chinese have responded differently (Shah et al 2004). Like in SSP, in many Chinese irrigation systems, while the state built the main canals and branches, village collectives were required to build the local distribution system. Like in the SSP command, most village collectives did not build their distribution systems. As a result, many canal systems release water in a medium sized reservoir from where water is conveyed by canals into ditches, from which irrigators lift water. Besides the lifting costs, farmers have to pay for water too, as is envisaged in the SSP. But collecting water fees is as difficult there as it is here; and so is enforcing the rule that the user pays and the non-payer does not use. In China's volumetric pricing system, we found constant measurement is not done, yet some of the gains of volumetric charge are reaped. The engineer in charge of a reservoir with say 25 million m3 of water capable of serving an irrigation area of say 8,000 ha, is given an incentive on his fee collection performance. In small systems we saw in Hebei and Hanan provinces in north China, a standard loss allowance at 25 percent was provided to cover seepage and conveyance losseds. So the incentive available to the official—over and above his salary is 10 percent of the excess of total water fee collected, less the base value of 75 percent of the dynamic storage in the reservoir, costed at the government-fixed water rate per cubic meter. Rough calculations showed that the total incentive earned is no more than 30-35 percent of the regular pay; yet, it generated accountability and efficiency we normally do not find in bureaucratic systems. There is growing evidence that this system has been working quite well in China.

Another alternative is to institute private franchises. YK Alagh has for long talked about a corporation for each of the Narmada branches. But a simpler idea is to invite private local entrepreneurs—as concessionaires or franchise holders—to bid for water transmission and fee collection from WUAs. If this is to work well, franchise operators will need to have a medium to long-term stake; however, contracts can be suitably designed to protect the interest of the SSP, franchise holders as well as farmers.

In our view, what is critical at this stage of the SSP is not the total amount of revenue the project generates or collects, or the total area it covers: but the firm establishment of the basic rules of the game, which in our opinion should be five: *(a)* SSP will provide assured irrigation in specified quantity at pre-announced scheduled; *(b)* it will receive indents for irrigation only from water user associations and not from individual members; *(c)* it will not supply water to any WUA unless it has deposited the water fee in advance; *(d)* once the irrigation starts, anybody who has not indented or paid for water will not make commitments to farmers that it cannot keep, and if commitment are made, they will be kept at any cost. If these basic rules of the game are not established now, the SSP will most likely go the way other irrigation projects have.

9

Management of Large Irrigation Projects in India

North Gujarat is naturally endowed with one of the riches alluvial aquifers of India but its uncontrolled exploitation for irrigation has resulted in many undesirable consequences. A major hydrological opportunity for rejuvenation of the aquifer system is provided by the availability of unutilized flows from Narmada basin. It is proposed to divert this water to north Gujarat through the Narmada main canal, and use the existing canal networks and village ponds and tanks in the region to activate a decentralized recharge process. This paper examines its physical and economic feasibility. And evaluation of two recharge scenarios in north Gujarat shows that using pumped water for recharging outside the designated command area may prove to bean uneconomical proposition, unless there is substantial increase in the productivity of water. Recharge within the command would be much more economical.

The presence of rich and extensive alluvial aquifers and a highly enterprising farming community had made the semi-arid and otherwise dry north Gujarat region the centre of agricultural growth in the state for the past four decades. But the region's groundwater resources are now under great stress, manifested in rapidly falling water levels and deteriorating water quality. The reason for the genesis of north Gujarat's groundwater crisis has been its intensive use for irrigated farming, which is out of balance with its natural replenishment from rainfall. The tube wells and open wells in north Gujarat pump out about 3000 million cubic metres (mcm) of groundwater annually against an annual replenishment of nearly, 2400 mcm, resulting an annual deficit of about 600 mcm. The direct cost of groundwater depletion to the economy is an area of grave concern to the state government, which subsidises electricity use in north Gujarat's well irrigation to the tune of Rs. 300 crore per year. For formers too, agriculture is becoming increasingly un profitable because of high costs of groundwater irrigation in spite of the highly subsidized electricity used for lifting water (IRMA 2001).

In the past, numerous ideas of water transfers were floated the bais of all of which was the uneven distribution of resource endowment across the state. The mean annual rainfall in the state varies from 350 mm in Kachchh to nearly 2000 mm in the Dangs district in south Gujarat. Closer think, and Khemabai Patel, a farmer leader of Sbakantha, to link the hydrologic systems of north and south Gujarat to reduce water stress in the former (Shaha 1998). The Sardar Sarovar development plan itself had envisaged that water pumped downstream of the main dam, after use in power generation would be supplied to three major and nine medium irrigation projects in north Gujarat, to augment their water storage capacity and thus provide security to about 2.3 lakh ha irrigated land under these schemes (GoG 1989). A water resource planning exercise done by Tahal Consulting Engineers for the government of Gujarat examined the possibility of artificial recharge of aquifers in north Gujarat, and recommended the use of imported water from Narmada for recharge by spreading methods in upper regional aquifers and riverbeds (GoG 1996).

With the Sardar Sarovar dam height reaching a stage where it is possible to divert water into the main canal, the idea of water import now seems to be becoming a reality. As the utilization potential created within the designated sectors, particularly irrigation, is going to remain far less than the planned utilization in the next few years, tremendous scope exists for using this water for ecological purposes, such as recharging north Gujarat's depleted aquifers. While the present interventions proposed by the government seem to bead hoc, they can have potential long-term positive impact son the socio-economic condition of the communities and environment, if carried out systematically. The objective of thus study is to examine the physical and economic feasibility of using Narmada water for recharging north Gujarat aquifers through analyses of two recharge options.

As the agricultural demand for water underwent an exponential growth in north Gujarat during 1960-1990, there was an explosion of tube wells powered by high capacity pump sets to meet this demand, as surface water supplies were extremely limited. While irrigated agriculture flourished, groundwater draft far exceeded the recharge. It shows taluk-wise figures of the stage of groundwater development in north Gujarat, as per the estimates of the government of Gujarat (GoG 1999). As compared to the rest of Gujarat, north Gujarat, has a significantly larger proportion of talukas classified as 'over-exploited' and 'dark'

Over-exploitation of groundwater had caused dying up of open wells and dug-cum-bored wells in alluvial parts of north Gujarat. Falling groundwater table had not only resulted in an increase in the capital cost of tube well construction but also added to variable costs of energy used for lifting water and well maintenance. The costs of irrigation in north Gujarat amount to about 36 percent of total input costs, with the result that the net return per unit land for crops such as wheat and cotton remains the lowest in comparison to other regions of Gujarat (for wheat and cotton, IRMA 2001).

This dismal groundwater situation is accentuated by the inherently poor surface water resources of the region. Rivers in north Gujarat flow from the hilly region in the northeast towards the Gulf of Khambat or the Rann of Kachchh. They are seasonal in nature, carrying stream flows only during three to four months of the year. The rivers experience high variability in their annual flows and are mostly dry during low rainfall years (Kumar 2002; 19) the major and medium irrigation schemes in north Gujarat were designed for run-off very low dependability and hence their performance is highly susceptible to run-off variability. Due to over-appropriation of run-off, in most yeas there is no spillover from these reservoirs into the downstream (Kumar 2002). In April 2000, as against the total capacity of 2018 mcm in 13 major and minor dams of north Gujarat, the storage available was only about 6 mcm. Records for three reservoirs in north Gujarat, viz., Hathmati, Meshwo and Dantiwada, show that the reservoirs have been filled to less than 50 percent of their capacity for almost half the yeas under study (GoG 1989:437). To sum up, any further surface water development of significant scale in north Gujarat using native water does not seem possible, and astute management of groundwater seems to be the only way to ensure sustained availability of water in region.

Potential Link between Narmada Canal and Hydrologic System of North Gujarat

The designated command area of the Sardar Saovar Project (SSP) in north Gujarat covers only a small portion of arable land and approximately 14 percent of the geographical are of the region. Irrigation water will be supplied by the Kachchh branch canal that will supply water to areas in the western pats of Banaskantha and Mehsana districts, falling on the western bank of the main canal. But the alluvial aquifers of north Gujarat, which experience over-draft conditions, have a larger aerial extent and spread far beyond the designated command areas to cover the northeastern side of the main canal.

Therefore, a conjunctive management system to transfer Narmada water to north Gujarat and then to recharge the aquifers in a decentralized way would be independent of the irrigation canal network since most of this water import would be carried out on the eastern bank, which lies outside the command. Early plans pertaining to the use of excess water from the Sardar Sarovar dam envisaged the lifting of water from a single point along the main canal to reservoirs in the northern hills such as Dharoi, Dantiwada and

Sipu through a series of pumping stations. The present modified plan, tentative in nature, envisages the establishment of four pumping stations along the main canal to lift water rinto50 large tanks situated in the vicinity of the canal, and its subsequent transport to approximately 4000 ponds of north Gujarat in addition to large and medium dams. Some pertinent questions related to this issue are given below.

Is There Enough Narmada Water for North Gujarat's Aquifers?

The Government of Gujarat estimates of groundwater recharge, draft and deficit in north Gujarat are dealing. A comparison of the volumetric deficit of groundwater with volumes of possible recharge of Narmada water will indicate the extent to which recharge can reverse the trend of groundwater declines.

In total groundwater deficit (Difference between annual utilizable recharge and annual daft) is 562.39 mcm, say 600 mcm. We have considered a gross draft) is 562.39 mcm, say 600 mcm. We have considered a gross annual water requirement for induced recharge required to the tune of 1,000 mcm. The additional 400 mcm water in excess of the annual groundwater deficit is to take care of the mining of deep aquifers that due to the accumulated historical deficits.

Availability of run-off water for supply to north Gujarat will be subject to the availability of flows in the Narmada at the sadar Sarovar dam site, and in excess of Gujarat's allocation of about 11100 mcm (9.0 maf). There is no allowance from Gujarat's allocated volume for ecological uses such as recharging depleted aquifers. Apart from 1300 mcm allocated for domestic and industrial use, the remaining 9800 mcm will be diverted to irrigating areas in the designed command area on a priority basis. Hence all flows that have to be diverted to north Gujarat will have to be sourced from excess water that will be available at the Sardar sarovar dam, mainly during the monsoon.

North Gujarat's recharge requirement of 1000 mcm is volumetrically equivalent thoroughly 10 per cent of Gujarat's allocation of 11100 mcm. For the inflow at SSP to provide an excess volume of 1000 mcm, an annual yield to the tune of 35,500 mcm would be required, considering a total allocation of 34500 mcm of water from the basin to the beneficiary states. Plotting annual inflows based on inflow series for 1891-1990 shows that the probability of annual run-offs exceeding 35500 mcm is 70 per cent; i e, in 70 out of 100 years, adequate excess flows to the tune of 1000 mcm would be available.

There could be significant reductions in the probability of the occurrence of such a flow if the recent hydrological trend in Narmada basin with regard to stream flows is to continue [See Kumar et al; 2004a for details of basin hydrology]. Nevertheless, at least for the next couple of decades, the figures of excess flowered out by us would not be an overestimate. This is because our calculations assume that Madhya Pradesh would soon start utilizing its allocation of 22500 mcm of water from Narmada and for this to happen the entire Narmada valley development plan, comprising 29 major, 135 medium and 3500 minor dams upstream of the Sardar Sarovar dam, have to be executed. Till that conditions reached, an availability of excess flow will be more than those depicted by the figure of 70 per cent reliability.

Is There Sufficient Storage and Recharge Infrastructure in North Gujarat?

We need to examine the availability of sufficient storage space in large reservoirs and village ponds to assess their ability to detain the incoming flows before they get recharged; there are a large number of reservoirs constructed in north Gujarat, mainly in the basins of Sabarmati, Banas and Saraswati. Records of three reservoirs in north Gujarat, namely, Hathmati, Meshwo and Dantiwada, show that the reservoirs have been filled to less than 50 per cent of their capacity for almost half the years under study [GoG 1989:437]. This indicates the presence of good storage potential for imported water. Table 4 shows storage volumes of large dams and village tanks in north Gujarat. It can safely be assumed that baring high rainfall years, 25 per cent capacity of large and small reservoirs; i.e., 1000 mcm will be available for storage of imported water.

The geo-hydrological conditions in north Gujarat are highly conducive to artificial recharge of groundwater. Further, soils in north Gujarat have high permeability and infiltration capacity. With an annual groundwater recharge rate of 0.106 mcm/sq km, recharge rates are high for the medium rainfall the region receives. There are two major aquifer units in the area—the upper unit being mostly unconfined with a thickness of 35 m to 125 m and the lower unit with alternate layers of clay and sand being generally confined in nature and found up to a depth of 600m. Evaluation of various recharge techniques was carried out as part of artificial recharge study done by UNDP (1986) in Mehsana which showed that artificial recharge to the upper unconfined aquifer was feasible by spreading methods such as spreading channels, recharge pits and ponds. Tests found infiltration rates of 19 cm/day to 96 cm/day, with higher infiltration rates being observed in areas where the water table was deeper unsaturated zones more permeable. Long-term recharge tests on desalted ponds showed groundwater mounds of a few 1000 sqkm areas and height of 10 to 18 m.

Considering a long-infiltration rate of 30cm/day recharge from 4000 ponds in north Gujarat well a constant supply of water for 120 days can effectively recharge a volume of 1440 mcm. This shows the feasibility of using surface spreading methods to recharge the unconfined alluvial aquifers.

Analysis of Economic Aspects of Recharge Scenarios

From the point of view of groundwater recharge from SSP north Gujarat can be divided into two areas: *(i)* the area lying on the west bank of the Narmada Main Canal (NMC) in the designated command area of SSP, which is 4500 sq km in area, and *(ii)* the area lying on the east bank and outside the command area of SSP, which is 23500 sq km in area. While both areas share a similar hydro geological profile and groundwater availability, the system of recharge and its economics in these two parts will be vastly different.

Recharge in the area lying in the designated command area of the SSP can be achieved by transferring water to about 800 ponds through a feeder network, which can be drawn form the planned canal network in the command. It is estimated that 200 mcm of water can be diverted and stored in these local storages for recharge purposes. Transferring water to non-command areas to the east of the NMC will be a much more expensive exercise, since it will require dedicated pumping and conveyance infrastructure to convey water from lifting points along the NMC to 14 large dams and about 3200 village ponds lying in this area.

The economic viability of both these recharge scenarios has been evaluated on the basis of the economic cost of irrigation with recharged water, taking into account both costs of transferring water from NMC, recharging and subsequent withdrawal for irrigation. The present economic value of groundwater use in irrigated agriculture exclusive of irrigation costs and incisive of all other input costs, has been estimated to be 3.14rs/m3 on the basis of estimates provided in Kumar et al (2004b). Economic analysis has been done separately for each scenario. Scenario 1 indicates recharge in the command area and Scenario 2 represents recharge in the non-command area.

The actual economic cost of transferring and recharging imported water has been estimated on the basis of depreciation on capital cost of infrastructure; and variable costs of staffing, repaid and maintenance, energy used for lifting water and de-silting of reservoirs and ponds for efficient recharge. While the capital cost infrastructure in Scenario 2 is taken as Rs. 2500 crore no capital cost is considered in Scenario 1 as under this scenario, the infrastructure already being constructed under SSP will be used for recharge activities. The cost of abstraction of groundwater is considered on the basis of the assumption that recharge to the prelatic aquifer will create substantial increases in groundwater levels and allow access to groundwater through shallow dug wells, thus reducing energy costs of extraction significantly. Cost of abstraction taken here is no the assumption of 5 HP pumps being used for abstraction.

Economic cost of recharge in the command area of SSP (Scenario 1) is justified in view of the present economic vale of groundwater irrigation which is 3.41Rs/m3 in comparison to cost of groundwater which is 1.95 Rs m3 However, cost of recharge outside the command area (Scenario 2) which requires lifting up to a height of 75 m shows itself to be economically unviable in view of the high cost of groundwater.

Conclusions

Our evaluation of the induced recharge of north Gujarat aquifers using Narmada water covered two recharge scenarios: *(i)* recharge in the command area of SSP without lifting and *(ii)* recharge outside command area with lifting. It show s that recharging aquifers in the command area seems to be a variable proposition from an economic perspective if that addition recharge is to be diverted for irrigation. Using lifted water for recharge in the non-command areas, on the other hand, seems unviable when its cost is compared against the incremental value of the output that would be generated from its use. But it is important to note here that the full economic value of groundwater is not realized at present owing to farmers not being confronted with the real marginal cost of using electricity for lifting groundwater, which we have considered for estimating the cost of groundwater. The farmers currently pay for electricity used in groundwater pumping on the basis of pump horsepower rather than the actual number of units consumed, which makes the marginal cost of pumping groundwater near to zero. That said, once marginal cost is induced through appropriate pricing policies, the farmers might actually go for economically efficient crops thereby increasing the marginal value product of groundwater.

While alternatives to the lifting exercise envisaged in Scenario 2 may be difficult to conceptualize, it can be argued that a change in the mode of pricing electricity and volumetric rationing of recharged water may force farmers to sift to more economically efficient crops (from the point of view of water use) and close the gap between cost and economic value of recharged groundwater. Again, we have not considered the economic value of the social and environmental costs of groundwater depletion and increased public health costs associated with groundwater contamination, which need to be treated as benefits of equal magnitude, in the evaluation of cost and benefit s of recharge projects. Taking these benefits into account in the valuation process would strengthen the economic rationale for implementing Scenario 2.

10

Techniques of Water Pricing

Proper Pricing Policies is Needed

Clay (1974) found that payment for water was in cash at hourly rates. At that time (1971-73), groundwater markets were just emerging in the area. Therefore, the prevalence of cash transactions belies Shah's (1991) hypothesis that cash payment is indicative of a 'mature' stage of groundwater markets. Working in the same region 20 years later, Shah and Ballabh (1997) still found cash transaction was in vogue. However, working at around the same time in another region in neighbouring Bangladsh, Fujita and Hossian (1995) found that water sale through cash transaction accounted for only 3 percent of the total area irrigated through water markets, while most was accounted for by tenancy contracts between landowners and EMS owners. Lewis (1989) found that seasonal cash contract was the most important mode of transaction in the water market in the village he surveyed in Bangladesh. Pant (2003), Ballabh et al (2002) found conexistence of hourly cash and kind payments in many of there study villages. Based on a review of all these studies, it emerges that there can be two types of transactions in the water market: one is outright sale of water (against cash, kind or a mix of both, either at hourly or seasonal rates), and the second is some kind of tenancy arrangement under which the WEM owner can either lease in and from other landowners or lease out land in lieu of certain return, either fixed (in terms of money or in kind) or share of he produce. Dubash (2002), Aggarwal (1996) and Kajisa (1999) have explained such multiplicity of arrangements in terms of risk haring and reducing transaction costs while neoclassical economists have rejected these as a transitory phenomenon which they say will give way to cash transactions as markets mature. Table lists different modes of transactions and compares them against he stage of development of water markets and finds no particular relationship between the mode of payment and level of development of the groundwater market.

On the issue of water pricing, three types of concerns have been raised. First, whether or not water sellers exert monopoly powers to gain supernormal profits. Shah (1993) modeled groundwater markets as natural oligopolies, under which he hypothesized that the ratio of water charge (w) to total variable post (c) is a fairly good indicator of the level of monopoly profit. He also hypothesized that as the markets became more competitive (due to introduction of more WEMs or change in power riff), this ratio will fall steadily. In his and Ballabh's study of six villages in Muzaffarpur, they found that the water price was 2.5-3.0 times the incremental pumping costs. Clay, working in the same region roughly 30 years ago, found a w/c ratio of 2, which is more or less the same as reported by Shah. This temporal evidence questions Shah's hypothesis that as markets development, the w/c ratio comes down. On the other hand, while both Fujita and Hossian (1995) and Palmer-Jones (2001) found a fairly high w/c ratio in their study, unlike Shah they concluded that far from being monopolistic, water markets are competitive and a high w/c ratio merely reflects entrepreneurs' risk premium.

The second issue of enquiry is on the existence of price discrimination in water markets. Clay (1974) found a consistent pattern of price discrimination along the line that closely followed near relations and others. So did shah and Ballabh (1997), but they did not indicate if that had anything to do with the caste and status of the water buyer. But almost all others (Ballabh et al 2002; Pant 2003, Wood 1995) concede that discounts are generally given to kith and kin, though Lewis (1989) says that such discounts are not particularly common in the Bangladeshi village that he studied.

The third important issue is whether there is any causal relationship between monopoly rent, price discrimination and the level of development of groundwater markets. The neoclassical economists hypothesise that as markets develop and become more competitive, monopoly power of the water seller goes down. Compares the relationship between the extent of monopoly power and breadth and depth in six villages in north Bihar that Shah and Ballabh (1997) studied, and finds no clear-cut relationship between the level of development of groundwater markets and degree of monopoly pricing.

Literature is divided on the question of impact of

groundwater markets, ranging from highly positive ones that declare groundwater markets as the 'vehicle of poverty alleviation' to that that accuse groundwater markets of 'creating water lords' and appropriating surplus from the poor. There are two major ways in which the impact of groundwater market is manifested; first, in changes in cropping pattern and cropping intensity among the buyers and sellers, and second in terms of employment generation among the landless. The way these two variables are affected, in turn, affects the way net irrigation surplus (NIS) is distributed among WEM owners and water buyers.

One of the central arguments of the neoclassical scholars (Shah 1993; Shah and Ballabh 1997) is that the difference in crop productivity and cropping pattern among water sellers and water buyers is a good indicator of the level of development of water markets. This is because cropping decision and the resulting crop productivity under green revolution technology is a function of reliability and adequacy of irrigation water. If, under such circumstances, the water buyers achieve as good output as WEM owners, then it indicates water markets deliver reliable and adequate water to the buyers. Shah and Ballabh (1997) find that in all the six villages cropping intensity of the WEM owners and that of the water buyers are comparable. They also find that water buyers invariably achieve higher yields than water sellers and in some crops, such as potato, water buyers achieve nearly twice the output of water sellers. An AERC (1988) study finds that while cropping intensity of water buyers was higher than that of well owners (228 percent as against 205 percent), cropping pattern of the latter had much more area under water-intensive and profitable 'boro' paddy (36 percent) compared with water buyers, who could barely devote 7 percent of their area to boro cultivation. Thus, in this case, water buyers were at a positive disadvantage vis-à-vis water sellers.

As far as labour employment is concerned, there is enough evidence to show that employment goes up with the introduction of irrigated agriculture, but none except Shah and Ballabh (1997) and AERC (1998) compare the difference in labour employed between water sellers and water buyers. Shah and Ballabh found that water buyers spent more per acre on labour during the rabi season-which is the main irrigation season in the study villages, while the AERC study found no such difference. Clay (1974) compared the use of labour in agriculture before and after investment in tube well technology. He found, quite predictably, that labour use had gone up in the after-investment period is shown.

Though there is not an iota of doubt that groundwater markets increase, NIS, there is some controversy about the way this NIS is divided among the WEM owners, water buyers and labourers. Fujita and Hossain (1995) found that 20 percent of NIS went to the landowners who seasonally rented out land to tubewell owners under fixed tenancy arrangement, 15 percent went to water buyers and the rest 65 percent to WEM, while their respective landholding in the village was 42 percent, 24 percent and 35 percent. Thus, it is clear that the WEM owners captured the lion's share of NIS generated in their study village. On the other hand, Palmer-Jones (2001) observed that ". ...Most profits from irrigated agriculture accumulate to land owners rather than WEM owners" (p. 13), but he gave no quantitative validation of his argument.

Finally Clay (1974) found that with tubewell irrigation, the factor share of labour went down, though in absolute terms labour employment increased.

On the whole, based on the literature reviewed so far, water markets in the GMB basin do not seem to have any deleterious effect. On the contrary, they increase NIS through higher crop productivity and cropping intensity, lead to higher labour employment and in regions of water logging, it helps to stabilize water tables. Though formulation of water sellers as 'water lords' still remains quite popular, especially with the scholars of Marxian tradition (Wood 1995; Adnan 1999), no such concrete evidence is seen in any of the papers examined in this review. Given that much of eastern India has very small and fragmented landholdings, and that in order to break even, every WEM owner is dependent on the water buyer, and that the water seller in most instances is also a water buyer, tendencies leading to so call 'water lordism' are curbed. In addition, the shallow depths at which water is found and the relative ease with which tubewells can be sunk further limits the power of WEM owners.

Compared with other rural institutional arrangements such as land, labour and credit markets, the water market is a relatively recent field of enquiry. Since the mid 1980s, shah (1985, 1988, 1991 and 1993), through his pioneering work has more or less moulded the shape of discourse on water markets. His approach has been that of a neoclassical economist (NCE). On the other hand, Dubash (2000, 2002), Kajisa (1999) and Palmer-Jones (1994) have charted a different path along the lines of new institutional economics (NIE). In this section, I will look at the origin and postulates of the two approaches and review the main grounds on which they have been criticized.

During the mid-1980s, when shah stumbled upon the phenomenon of the groundwater market, there were increasing concerns about runaway growth in groundwater irrigation and inefficacy of any direct measures to regulate such growth. Given this background, he wanted to understand how indirect regulation could modify behaviour of water sellers (Shah 2004). In doing so, he modeled water markets as natural oligopolies and hypothesized that the mode of power tariff was the most important determinant of the level of vibrancy of water markets, and that a progressive flat tariff regime coupled with high quality power supply is conductive to the emergence of a competitive water market. His approach was highly policy-oriented.

But in recent years, this approach has come under increased criticism. For one, it is being questioned whether groundwater markets are indeed markets in neoclassical term. The first condition of same price for same commodity does not apply; different water sellers charge different water sellers charge different water prices by virtue of being located in different villages or even in the same village.

Second, different buyers buy water at the same price, but they get differential quality of service. Third, freedom for purchasers and sellers is not respected, it is controlled by the technical factors such as command area that the tube well can irrigate and whose land falls within that domain. In addition to this basis methodological dilemma, two more criticisms have been leveled against this approach. For one, it is largely assumed that individual actions are not constrained by social institutions or alliances such as caste, gender, kinship, decent line or residence group and this assumption is not true in most cases. Second, the role of power in shaping water markets has been completely ignored.

The other approach of studying water markets is that of NIE. In interpreting groundwater markets, the NIE approach has tried to show how water markets have emerged to share risks inherent in irrigated agriculture, given that there is an absence of insurance markets. Bubash (2000, 2002) has shown that groundwater markets are 'socially and ecologically 'embedded with a 'path dependent' history. Using this approach, one can indeed explain some of the unexplained facets, e.g., the coexistence of different modes of water contracts as strategies to minimize or share risks or lower transaction costs. This approach also sheds light on why the same set of policy interventions gives rise to different sets of outcomes. The main drawback of this approach is that it fails to generalize.

NCEs and NIEs ask two different sets of questions vis-à-vis water markets. The NCE's central concern is how water markets can be used as a level for managing groundwater economy, while the NIEs are more interested in understanding how water markets function as a social and economic institution. Then, are the approaches dichotomous? The so-called dichotomy, I believe, lies more in the scale of analysis. While the NCEs try to paint a macro-level picture, the NIEs are content with a micro-level image. Perhaps the reality lies midway. There are indeed certain core features of water markets that pervade across villages and regions, whereas there are other characteristics that are path dependent and hence vary from one village to another. Quite understandably, the best way to study water markets would be to combine both methods, which has not been done so far.

Future Policy Options

Being a relatively new field of study, certain glaring gaps have remained in the way water markets have been studied. First, there has been a regional bias, in that groundwater markets have been better studied in water scarce regions that in water abundant regions. Now the focus needs to be shifted to water abundant regions such as the GMB basin. Second, there has been a lack of historical perspective in groundwater market research. Questions such as 'is there as stage wise progression in the development of groundwater markets from one of underdevelopment to that of competitive markets?' and 'if yes, is such a progression smooth and unilinear?' have at best remained hypothetical. Third, the relation between development of groundwater markets and level of agricultural development have remained imperfectly understood. Only Shah (1997) has presented a simplified stage wise linear model of groundwater-led agrarian transformation in eastern India, much along the contours suggested by Rostow (1961), but its main limitation is that it does not explicitly include agrarian relation as a constraining factor. Fourth, the role of 'power' has been widely used to formulate theories on labour and credit markets. However, in the study of water markets, not much attention has been paid to the question of power in rural society; if at all, the formulation has been very naive and the water sellers have been depicted as 'water lords'—those who exert absolute power over water buyers (Wood 1995; Webster 1999). Only lewis (1989) observed that even water buyers could have power over the water sellers. More work needs to be done in understanding the relative power of water sellers and water buyers and how this in turn shapes water markets. Finally, unlike other rural markets, such as labour and credit, there has so far been no attempt at formulating a general theory of groundwater markets. Thus, the current mode of functioning of groundwater market still leaves a lot of unanswered questions such as 'why do several modes of water contracts coexist under seemingly similar conditions and why do why do they respond differently to similar sets of incentives and disincentives?' if not a coherent theory of water markets, what is at least needed is a formulation of 'core features' of groundwater markets similar to the core features of the labour market outlined by Dreze and Mukherjee (1987). The best way to do so would be to combine both the NCE and NIE perspective.

Given that water markets have assumed increased importance an the GMB basin and that the entire basin is in the throes of a major agricultural transition, there is an urgent need to understand the role that groundwater markets can play in this transition. In doing so, some of the points mentioned in this section could be kept in mind for a fuller understanding of the remarkable phenomenon that is the groundwater market.

Rejuvenating Irrigation Tanks through Local Institutions

Recent attempts to modernize irrigation tanks with a

focus on physical rehabilitation, but little institutional development to maintain and manage them, have resulted in a vicious cycle. With the lack of maintenance and upkeep, rehabilitated tanks soon fall into disrepair, necessitating a new round of externally induced rehabilitation. Yet, there are many tanks under traditional local management operating at a high level of performance equilibrium. A study of 41 tanks from 22 districts of eight Indian states was taken up under the IWMI-Tata programme to identify the characteristics of high performing local-managed tank institutions. The lessons learnt from the study can form the basis for an effective institutional protocol that can enhance the effectiveness of tank rehabilitation and modernization.

India's water resources potential and the country's agricultural economy hinge on the monsoon rains and its spatial and temporal variation. Nearly 40 per cent of India's land mass falls under semi-arid conditions with annual rainfall of 500-1000 mm and normal rainfall in necessary for a good crop. Facing high spatial and temporal variability of rainfall since time immemorial, India's rural communities have followed a policy of conserving rain water for subsequent use through innumerable tanks or small storage structures like ponds built, owned and managed by the local people through community organizations.

Tanks in the Indian context are inextricable linked to the socio-cultural aspects for rural life and have historically been an indispensable part of the village habitat, sustaining its socio-ecological balance. Tank systems, developed ingeniously and maintained over the centuries, have provided insulation form recurring droughts, floods, vagaries of the monsoon, and offered the much needed livelihood security to the poor living in fragile semi-arid regions. Of late, the importance of tanks is being realized even more, as the rapidly growing use of groundwater and large surface irrigation systems are proving costly and inadequate to meet the increasing demands for irrigation water. Conserving the tank eco-systems for multiple uses such as irrigation, domestic and livestock use and groundwater recharge is a way to provide a safety net to protect the livelihood of millions in a semi-arid India.

Status of Tanks in India

Almost all monsoon countries in the semi-arid tropics have small water bodies like tanks [Sengupta 1985]. In India, the largest concentration of tanks is found in the three southern states of Andhra Pradesh, Karnataka and Tamil Nadu and the union territory of Pondicherry, which account for nearly 60 per cent of India's tank-irrigated area. Out of India's 208000 tanks, theses states have nearly 120000 irrigating 1.8 million hectares of land [Vaidyanathan 2001].

The pre-eminence of tanks as a source of water storage and supply for multiple use was lost after independence due to a variety of factors: chiefly, the development of large-scale gravity irrigation systems, rapid spread of tube well technology, and decline in traditions of community management. As a result, a large majority of the tanks in the southern and eastern parts of India suffer from inadequate management and maintenance, some have become dysfunctional while others are even obliterated. In fact, even the exact number of tanks existing as of now and their stauts is not know [Pant 2004].

Tank Rehabilitation Programmes

In recent years, a variety of efforts have been made to improve the performance of tanks. One approach has been to seek external funds for the large investment needed to rehabilitate tanks systems and, thereafter, to encourage villagers to maintain it thorough the formation of tank water users' associations (WUAs). In Tamil Nadu, 569 public works department (PWD) tanks and 80 ex-zamin tanks (out of a total 39200 tanks) were rehabilitated and modernized under European Union assistance, with financial outlay of Rs. 179.39 crores. These tanks were supposed to benefit a command area of 73,161 ha and the cost of rehabilitation worked out to be Rs. 25,000/ha. An evaluation of the tank rehabilitation project by Anna University indicated that the outcomes were neither fruitful nor were the returns commensurate with the cost of rehabilitation. Because of inadequate institutional development and the piecemeal approach used for implementing the tank rehabilitation, the tanks fell into the vicious cycle of "rehabilitation-poor maintenance-deterioration-rehabilitation" [CWR 2000].

Similarly, Karnataka has recently taken up a much-needed initiative to rehabilitate 2000 minor irrigation tanks through the community based approach using World Bank funding. This project is under implementation of the last two years and yet to be evaluated, but a key emergent issue is the need to real with competing interests of stakeholder groups. A recent study on Rajasthan tanks found that no commonality of interests exists amongst key stakeholders groups of rehabilitated tanks: command area farmers, thank bed farmers, fishermen and the village community as a whole. Shah and Raju (1999) argue that the complex reality of tanks in Rajasthan today is perhaps the dialectic of opposing stakeholder priorities, hence the low-level performance equilibrium in which tanks is trapped today. They emphaised that a radical and effective institutional solution needs to be found to increase the performance of rehabilitated tanks. There is prevalent notion among a section of researchers and policy-makers that the present method of rehabilitating tanks and creating water user' associations is not the right water to improve the gross tank product per cubic meter of tank water. A drastic change is needed in the thinking on, and implementation of tank rehabilitation.

Why a Study on Tank Institution is Needed

Traditional tank institutions have undergone changes because of the vast increase in the number of irrigators, shifts in control of the land from a few to many landowners, changes in the attitude of farmers, and the spread of well irrigation in tank commands. A key question in today's changed context is: is it possible to create a new relationship between tanks and tank communities such that tanks play a more purpose full role of enhanced value creation for all stakeholders? [Shah 2003].

The overarching hypothesis of this research is that it is possible to build such a new relationship. Lessons for how best to do this can be gleaned by studying the experience of many tank communities with traditional institutions which still manage tanks effectively as common property, despite the presence of many or all of the external factors that have led to a general decline of tanks. It was in this context that a research study was taken up under the IWMI-Tata programme to identify the characteristics of high performing local managed tank institutions which are able to adept themselves to changes in water supply, groundwater development, changes in cropping pattern, and wider socio-economic changes such as changing landholding patterns, social structure, urbanization and others. Specific objectives of this research were: *(a)* understand the characteristics that a traditional tank institution should possess to perform at a high level of equilibrium; and *(b)* based on such understanding, to develop on institutional protocol for tank rehabilitation derived from the lessons learned form the case studies of high performing tank institutions.

As a part of this study, 41 tanks from 22 districts in eight states with command areas ranging from 50 to 1600 ha were studied. The tanks studied differed in their sources of water supply: rainfed (20), river fed (12) and rain fed cascades (9). They differed in their ownership pattern too by agencies such as zilla parishads, village panchayats, revenue department, PWD or minor irrigation department (MI) and village communities. At the time of the study, 27 tanks were used exclusively for irrigation; five tanks for fisheries; four for irrigation and fishery and five for other uses such as cattle drinking and groundwater recharging. The tanks studied were managed by a variety of institutions: traditional (10), traditional and registered (5), registered WUAs (17), fishermen cooperatives (5) and informal (4). These institutions were of different vintage: some were just four years old; some other had survived for more than 100 years.

Performance evaluation to assess the sustainability level of a tank institution is not easy. Therefore, a set of indicators were developed-from among several variables identified to have some bearing on tank performance—that contribute to understanding the overall performance of tanks. Each indicator contains finer components of several variables and all are given equal weights. A subjective score in the four-point scale (0 to 3) given by the field researcher is used for valuation of the indicatory. Based on the six indicators, an overall performance indicator was also developed. The following six indicators are scored for each tank.

Institutional Performance: Measured by the structure and composition of the tank user's group; their decision-making process; effectiveness in augmenting thank storage; rules and tools for operation and maintenance; conflict resolution procedure; the institution's ability to make plans according to water availability so as to provide social safeguards against water scarcity; avenues of resource mobilization, and interventions undertaken for improving the tank performance.

Tank contribution to livelihood performance is assessed by people's dependency on the tank not only for irrigation, but also for other uses like fish rearing, cattle use, and domestic use. The use of the tank bed and adjoining `poromboke' (wasteland for vegetable cultivation, tree cultivation, fuel wood cultivation, cattle grassing and employment generation); women's representation in the institution; non-farm activities relating to tank use, and tank water scarcity forcing migration were considered.

Enabling Conditions: Factors such as the socio-economic condition of villagers, favourable hydrology to ensure adequate water to the tank, eviction of tank bed and supply channel encroachment, cooperative ethos within the community, infrastructure development and access to the markets, employment generation and reinvestment of net income in agriculture were collected and used for computing the enabling environment performance.

Agricultural Performance: The success of an irrigation institution depends on its capability to bring water, manage it effectively and distribute it equitably. To measure these functions, the increase in agricultural production, increase in area irrigated, income generated and development of other associated non-farm activities were recorded.

Objective-Based Impacts: The impact of the performance of its objectives. Successful tank institution strives to conserve water to enable multiple uses. The productivity per unit of water must increase. Successful agricultural practices were identified together with employment generation and the re-investment of net income in agriculture by the tank users. All these factors were measured to assess the impact performance.

Institutional Sustainability: The sustainability performance of a tank institution is measured in terms of leadership; adequate water supply; rules and tools and powers to impose sanctions; support from other development agencies including the government; conflict resolution process; and role of traditional village council.

Each of the 41 tank case studies taken up under this study were evaluated in terms of the above indicators for them overall performance and the results were analyzed to identity high and low performing tanks and to explore the factors that explain high and low performance.

Water Acquisition

Availability of water is one of the most important factors determining tank performance. Tanks get water from rain, jungle streams or river diversion channels. Tank water acquisition is considered the most important function of the traditional institution. The study shows that each of the best performing tanks has its own techno-institutional mechanism for water acquisition.

In high performing tanks, such as Parambu tank in Pudukkottai district of Tamil Nadu, Kasargatte Hosa Anakere in Bangalore rural district of Karnataka, it was made mandatory for all able-bodied persons to participate in cleaning the feeder channels. Those who could not participate were required to pay the wages of labourers engaged as a substitute. In river-fed Rettaikulam tank in Thiruvelveli district of Tamil Nadu, the village committee engages wage labourers and watchers to clean the feeder channel and bring water, and paid them from their common found. In Pagadikulam tank in Dindigul district and Thamaraikulam in Theni district of Tamil Nadu, there are exclusive field level functionaries called the 'Kaval' agents to bring water from the river. The 'ooru panchayat' (traditional village council) of Hirekere in Tumkur district of Karnataka negotiates frequently with upstream tank farmers to get water for their tank during times of scarcity. When the Kedar tank in Villupuram district of Tamil Nadu was rehabilitated during 1990-92 under an EEC project, the farmers of the upstream tank wanted the Kedar farmers to do repairs and improvement works for their feeder channel. To get reliable water for the tank, upstream tank channel cleaning is important: keeping this in mind, the Kedar farmers allocated funds for channel cleaning of the upstream tank curtailing some of the works into heir own tank. The village committee in Katasunibandha tank in Dhenkanal district of Orissa created new channels to harvest more rainwater form the watershed through the shramdan of the villagers. The Villagers of Puseri in ramamnathpuram district of Tamil Nadu used to build a mud 'korambu (bund of earth mixed with paddy straw) in the river to divert water through group effort for more than 50 years. In an attempt to help the villagers, the government constructed a bed dam at the offtake point, from then on. The villagers stopped korambu formation but the dam was not built to sufficient height to head up water. The lack of inflow of water into the tanks encouraged people to encroach into the foreshore areas of the tank bed. The supply channels were encroached, too. Only rain-fed cultivation is now followed. A similar situation is observed in Najure tank in Pudukkottai district of Tamilnadu. The villagers had encroached everywhere including the feeder channels.

Since the encroachers either belong to the same village or family, it often becomes difficult to evict them and this has commonly lend to the total neglect of supply channels in many tanks. Pudukulam's surplus course that feeds Nanjure tank has been encroached for 30 years. The villagers are unable to evict these resulting in poor inflows to the tank. When the community is unable to prevent or overcome encroachment of supply channels the tank institution becomes inactive and dysfunctional.

Water Allocation and Distribution

Once the water is received in the tank it has to be distributed equitably to the satisfaction of all stakeholders. The village institution of Parambu tank in Pudukkottai district of Tamil Nadu has a slab system for distribution of water during scarcity. The system works in the following way:

(i) Farmers owning land up to one acre in the command area are permitted to cultivate their entire holding.

(ii) Farmers owning land between 1-5 acres in the command area are permitted to cultivate only half of their land holding area.

(iii) Farmers owing more than five acres int eh command area are permitted to cultivate only one third of their extent of holding.

The slab system is strictly enforced from the nursery stage of paddy itself. Water from the tank will be supplied to meet the requirement of paddy crop within the slab limits. If the storage in the tank is very low even to plan the slab system, the association decides not to supply water for the season. In Kongudi tank of Pudukkotai district of TamilNadu when the tank has inadequate storage, farmers who own less than 33 cents of land will get irrigation for their entire land. Others get water in a fixed proportion to their landholding decided by the *ambalams* (Village leaders) in the meeting. It is ensured that each one gets adequate water to raise a paddy crop at least on a portion of their land so that nobody in the village goes without some harvest to sustain their livelihood. Like in Kongudi in Sardarnagar taluk in Bhilwara district, Rajasthan, if the tank is not full, the entire command cannot be irrigated. In such a situation, water is given to each beegha' of land, irrespective of the farmer's holdings. Thus everybody receives minimum irrigation and food security is ensured. In the Hirekere tank in Karnataka, the command area is divided into three blocks based on the location, soil quality and area. When the tank is two-third full, only one block will get irrigation and when the tank is full, the water is provided to two blocks. At no time are all three blocks irrigated in a year due to paucity of water. These three blocks are irrigated in rotation, depending on the availability of water and as decided by the village institutions.

In Kedar, during the scarcity period, tank water is given only to those who do not have wells. In Sundarapandiapuram in Thirunelveli district of Tamil Nadu, when there was a drought for three years, only 'mettumadais' (elevated sluices) were opened and the ayacut under pallamadai (deeper sludices) had to depend on groundwater only. In Jetti Agrahara, in Tumkur district of Karnataka, only one crop is allowed to be cultivated normally. The remaining water is kept as dead storage for livestock. Paddy is the main crop. If the tank is half filled, only garden lands are given water by collecting a fee from farmers. In case the rainfed paddy is already planted in the command area, one watering is given against a reduced fee.

In Bairwar tank in Tikamgarh district of Madhya Pradesh, one village functionary called 'amin' used to regulate the distribution of water from the tank. With the formation of a WUA member. He opens the sluice only when he needs water. Only after he irrigates his field, other farmers are allowed to take water. Obviously the performance of Bairwar tank has deteriorated.

Decision Making

The functioning of successful traditional institutions

indicated a decision-making process, which involved all the stakeholders, and where the decisions made are accepted by all as fair. The Athoor Pattadhars Committee (Pagadaikulam) in Dindigul district of Tamil Nadu is functioning for the past 60 years; the tank ayacut and feeder channel are divided into kandams' (zones). The landholders in these zone belong to predominantly Christian, Hindu and Muslim religions. The office bearers of the farmers association are elected form these religions in rotation. The respective religious leaders also appoint irrigation functionaries from each zone.

In Kongudi in Pudukkottai district of Tamil Nadu, all major decisions are taken in a meeting where representatives of all the families are present. If any representative is occupied, he must inform village leaders and the meeting will be postponed. If anybody remains absent in a meeting without prior leave, the meeting gets postponed but the absentee pays a fine of Rs. 100. Unless everyone attends no decision is taken. In Arumugamangalam tank in Thoothukudi district of Tamil Nadu, all-important decisions are taken by the general body as a consensus decision. The executive committee looks after the implementation and day-to-day administration only. Many youth attend the meetings and actively take part in the Sangam's activities. The elders including the president and office bearers accept the views of the younger generation or try ot convince them to arrive at a consensus decision. The Peikulam tank institution in Thoothukudi district of Tamil Nadu was started in the year 1872 and continues to function smoothly. People from 16 villages were the first members. The rules governing the working of the institution—which are elaborate and interesting—were printed in July 1913. For instance, representation to all villages and hamlets were given in the executive committee. This association has been maintaining minutes of its meetings since 1872. There are written documents of all its activities and are open to anyone who would care to go through them. This transparency and collective decision-making have kept the institution vibrant for more then 130 years.

Thank institutions that lack cohesiveness or are non-inclusive or faction-ridden result in low performance. The Aralikkottai village council in sivagangai district of Tamil Nadu has representation form all castes except scheduled castes (SC). The people belonging to SC are not involved in the decision-making process in tank related issues due to caste discrimination. Elders from each caste group form the power centre in the village council and they make all the decision. The traditional association of Pappaiyanpatti village in Theni district of Tamil Nadu was virtually the big landowners association belonging to dominant castes of Naidus, Kallars and Vellalas, excluding others. These landowners still wield considerable influence in the affairs of the newly formed association. The dominant members take decisions and others are obliged to accept. In Dongargaon in Chandrapur district of Maharashtra state, three institutions are involved in the management of the tank: the Water Distribtuion Panch Committee (EDPC) fishermen's society and farmer community. They do not see eye to eye with one another; and none of them bother about augmenting tank storage while the cultivator community is plagued by factionalism. Obviously Aralikkottai, Pappaiyanpatti, and Dongargaon tank are not performing well.

Enforcement of Rules and Punishment of Violators

The rules once made have to be enforced and high performing tan institutions empower their agents to do this. There are tow types of irrigation functionaries in traditional institutions. One is at a more supervisory level as a decision-making and an enforcing authority and, the other, at a lower level involved in implementing and monitoring. In some systems, there are exclusive functionaries to implement the decisions and monitor them. The first type is called Nattamaikar, Patel or Kavaimaniam. The second level or irrigation workers are known by many names, Neerkatti Neergandi, Neerpaichi, Kanduvetti Kambukatti, Kavalar Shena, Thotti, Shnbog and Soudi. In all the tank systems that we found high performing, no farmer is permitted to operate the sluices. This task is entrusted to functionaries appointed for irrigation management who may hold the post on a hereditary basis or temporarily for a period ranging from a month to a year.

The Jetti agrahara village in Karnataka has a unique system of nominating the Ejaman Panakara ('patron') to coordinate the water distribution from the tank and its operation and maintenamce on behalf of the grama sabha and *Achukattudarars*—or the *ayacutdaars*. It is an honorary post to which appointment is made by a grama sabha representing all villages in the tank command (two persons from each village). The individual's skills in managing the communities is the key criterion and not the caste or landholding he posses. The appointment is an honour and imparts to the appointee a special social status and gives him the confidence to strictly enforce rules without fear or favour. Ejaman Panakkara has to mobilize *achumatudarars*, maintain the attendance for *shramadan* and take note of the absentees. He has to maintain records such as the area covered under de-silting. A wide range of penalties attends the defaulters-from stern warnings to imposition of fines and, in the extreme, to stopping water supplies all together (Parambu, Kedar, sundarapandipuram tends in Tamil Nadu). More than the amount of fine imposed, is the social stigma attached to the punishment – the shaming involved—that acts as a powerful deterrent?

Mobilizing Financial Resources

Mobilizing financial resources is an important activity in the working of any institution. All the institutions we studied collect subscriptions through the sale of fishing rights, and of usufructs, and fines and fees from members. When these finds are inadequate to meet the operating cost, successful tank institution manages additional funds through innovative methods. The Rettaikulam tank in Thirunelveli district of Tamil Nadu a varitety of such innovative ideas. They levy 'Ayacut (tax on area commanded) a tax based on landholding and depending upon the extent of repair and maintenance work and the deficit in the fund, the tax rate per acre is decided. Five years the whole inlet channel to the tank wad de-silted and the (locally called 'Kattamanakku') weeds were cleared. This work was completed in 36 days with an expenditure of Rs. 2.75 lakh. For this work, a tax was collected from all the well owners at Rs. 500 per well. This fund was collected not only form the owners of wells in the ayacut area but also form those in the area—ayacut area. The well owners in this village had the connection that unless the tank got water their wells will go dry and, therefore, they were willing to pay the tax.

All agricultural products are sold thorough a commission agent. This commission agent is selected through an open auction by the committee. Farmers cannot sell their products to others and so other agent can make procurements from this village. From this auction the Rettaikulam Committee receives around Rs. 2 lakh per year. Another innovation is the appointment of the milkman. Most households keep cows to produced milk for household needs as well as for the market: milk is collected twice a day for procurement by the milk cooperatives. As each household cannot have a standard measuring vessel, there were many quarrels and conflicts. The committee decided to appoint milkman and provided standard measuring vessels approved by the government authorities. For each litre of milk collected, the households have to pay the milkman Rs. 0.20. And through the auction of the annual right form for milk collection form the village, the committee received Rs 89,000.

Lessons Learnt

The important functions of any irrigation institution as stated above are. Water acquisition, water allocation and distribution, resource mobilization, operation and maintenance, decision-making, enforcement of decisions and conflict resolution. An organization must be vibrant and energetic to perform these tasks. How these functions are performed, who plans and who implements decisions, what rules and tolls are used to plan and implement set the high performing tank institutions apart from the rest.

In the case of water acquisition, the case studies indicate that successful local institution adopts many ways to augment water supplies for their tanks. Hence, wherever the organization is able to ensure water supplies to the tanks by utilizing the collective effort of villagers or by the functionaries to the organization themselves, they perform well.

High performing tank institutions have well-defined norms, evolved over a long period of time, about allocation of water to various segments and special rules in times of scarcity. Tanks are common property of the village, and whether the institution makes provisions during a scarcity situation to enable economically weaker sections and the landless to sustain their livelihood, is an important factor in obtaining cooperation form all villagers. Though based on custom and tradition, they are clear, specific detailed and accepted by all *ayacutdaars* as fair. There are a wide range of allocation rules, which focus on ensuring livelihood to the marginal and poor.

Traditional institutions often exert control over crops grown and the area cultivated to match water availability. This is not merely distributing scarcity among all, but a prudent way of ensuring social justice. By such planning, all the farmers are sure of harvesting a successful crop at least in part of their land. The maximization of crop production during good years and minimization of losses in bad years are ensured by the collective decision made by traditional tank institutions.

The direct involvement of tank users in major collective decisions is important to ensure that the decisions reflect their interest and needs. One way to achieve this is to allow all the tank users to get involved in major decisions concerning the tank and its water resources. The decision-making process in the best performing institutions is characterized by transparency, involvement of all, accountability, fairness and equity, and avoidance of conflicts. Even the election process of the office bearers ensures the participation of al members. Wherever transparency, involvement of all in decision-making and accountability are absent, the performance of the tank is poor.

After making decisions it must be ensured that they are fully implemented and that free riding is prevented. But, individuals would have little incentive to comply with rules unless they believe their non-compliance will result in substantial penalty. In any tank systems, specialized monitors have been appointed to enforce rules. The tank institutions that have a mechanism of enforcing the rules and who penalize the violators create confidence among members. There may be some special cases where the rules have to be flexible, but agreed upon unanimously.

Traditional institutions are quick to grab any opportunity to adopt new and innovative methods of fund mobilization. There are no fixed rates at which contribution form members are raised; and the rate varies depending upon the maintenance needs. The revenue collected is generally more than sufficient to manage the affairs of the institution and it also used for village development activities. The villagers willingly contribute and defaults are rare.

Office-bearers vested with special prerogatives in rule formulation and enforcement are in a position to misuse their powers by framing and interpreting rules to their own advantage. Opportunistic behaviours by office-bearers is curbed by appointment of office-bearers through voting by water user's thus making these office-bearers answerable to water users. The best performing tanks have either a fixed tenure for their office bearers (in many tanks studied) or have recall powers for office bearer or functionaries.

Concluding Remarks

Despite several state-sponsored tank rehabilitation programmes in may states eh number of tanks rehabilitated effectively is negligible as compared to the total number of tanks. With limited water resources, vagaries of the monsoon and the looming water scarcity in many parts of India, water conservation and use by medium and micro water retaining structures have assumed greater significance, in this context tank renovation and rejuvenation with peoples' contribution is looked upon as cost effective, equitable and powerful tool to alleviate rural poverty. Restoring the physical conditions of tanks through rehabilitation and modernization is of course the necessary condition for doing this; but equally critical is to find ways and means to keep the modernized tanks in good conditions, on sustainable basis. Maintenance is the responsibility of both the government and the farmers. Without a well-defined programme to ensure this, the huge amount spent on physical rehabilitation will become fruitless after some years. An evaluation of the outcome of tank rehabilitation projects indicates that the importance given to structural improvements overshadows the institutional development [Sakthivadivel 2004]. Very little has been spend on institutional development. Tank performance cannot be improved by mere physical rehabilitation alone. For effective rehabilitation, the results of this research indicate that certain pre-conditions and requirements are to be met; these conditions and requirements then form the institutional protocol for future tank rehabilitation.

Ensuring Hydrological Adequacy: As water is the main concern of tank users and institutions, the availability of adequate water supplies to the tank is a pre-condition for taking up rehabilitation. Ensuring the presence of enabling conditions: External agencies –particularly the presence of enabling condition; external agencies particularly form the government-have to provide a supportive environment including help in removal and eviction of encroachment in the tank bed and supply channels. Encroachment of the tank bed and supply channels is the prime enemy of high performance of tanks in may parts of India.

Establishing Institutional Pre-condition: The lessons learnt from the case studies indicate that successful traditional tank institutions have certain characteristics and traits s with regard to carrying out water management functions, which makes them effective. These traits have to be present in the institutions if rehabilitation is to succeed. If they are absent, institutions with such traits have to be crafted and promoted before taking up physical rehabilitation. This requires that physical rehabilitation works be arcaded by an institutional protocol to ensure that institutional preconditions are created that will help the tank community to move to a higher trajectory of tank performance on a sustainable basis.

Institution building is along-term process requiring investment of resources and extensive trial and error. Tank communities should be made to perceive that the institutional changes contemplated would bring more benefits to them than potential costs. Only then there will be credible commitments and long-term cooperative relationships within the community.

Bibliography

Allan, T.J.A. (2003): 'Virtual Water-Problemshed Solutions for Water Scarce Watersheds: Consequences of Economic and Political Invisibility', [http://www.siwi.org/waterweek2003/ Workshop%207%20Oral(28).httm]

Areeparampil, M. (1996): *Tribals of Jharkhand: Victims of Development*, Indian Social Institute, New Delhi.

Agrawal, A. (2001): 'Common Property Institutions and Sustainable Governance of Resource', *World Development*, Vol. 29 (10): 1649-72.

Ballabh, Vishwa and Kameshwar choudhary (2003): Groundwater and Agriculture Production: A Comparative Study of Eastern UP, Bihar and West Bengal, IWMI-TATA Water Policy Programme, Anand.

Bhalla, G.S., P. Hazell and J. Kerr (1999): 'Prospects for India's Cereals Supply and Demand to 2020', 2020 Vision Discussion Paper 29. International Food Policy Research Institute (IFPRI), Washington, DC, November. [http://www.ifpri.org/2020/dp/dp29.pdf]

Bhamoriya, V. (2004): BAIF-DHRUVA Experience of enhancing tribal livelihoods in Navsari ad Valsad districts of South Gujarat. study under-taken as part of the ITP-SRTT Central India Initiative (CInI) and Paper presented at the CIOnI Synthesis Workship, Anand Gujarat, January 3-4.

Boserup, E. (1965): *The Conditions of Agricultural Growth,* George Allen and Unwin (reprinted in 1993 by Earthscan, London).

Batchelor, C., Rama Mohan Rao and Manohar Rao (2003): 'Watershed Development: A Solution to Water Shortages in Semi-Arid India or Part of the Problem?', LUWRR, 3, pp. 1-10.

CAG India (1982): *Development of Tube-well Irrigation in India,* Agricole Publishing Academy, New Delhi.

Chandrakanth, M.G., Bisrat, Alemu and Mahadev, G. Bhar (2004): 'Combating Negative Externalities of Drought—Goundwater Recharge Though Watershed Development programme,' *Economic and Political Weekly,* March 13, pp. 1164-70.

Farrington, J. (ed) (1999): *Participatory Watershed Management,* Oxford University press.

Godbole, Madhav (2002): 'Electricity Regulatory Commissions: The Jury Is Still Out', *Economic and Political Weekly,* Vol. XXXVII, No. 23, June 8-14, pp. 2195-2201.

James, A.J. (2003): 'Quantified Participatory Assessment of Project Impacts: the Western India Rainfed Farming Project II', DEFID India—Consultants' Report No: CR-67, New Delhi.

Kendy, E., T. Steenhuis and C Liu (2002): 'Policies Drain the North China Plain: Hydrologic Impacts of Institutional Changes Affecting Luancheng Country, Hebei Province, 1949-2000,' Department of Biological and Environmental Engineering, Riley Robb Hall, Cornell University, Ithaca NY. 14853, USA (Draft).

Kishore, A., A. Sharma and C. Scott (2002): Power Supply to Agriculture: Reassessing the Options, IWMI-Tata Water Policy Research Highlight No. 7.

Kurup, M.P.G. (2003): Livestock Policy Synthesis, Unpublished report prepared for the LEAD India Study, IWMI, Hyderabad.

Lohmar, Brian, Jinxia Wang, Scott Rozelle, Jikun Huang and David Dawe (2002): 'Investment, conflicts and Incentives: The Role of Institutions and Policies in China's Agricultural Water Management on the North China Plain', Agriculture Information Bulletin No 782. Economic Research Service, USDA.

India Task Force (1987): Report of the task Force to Evaluate Impact of Sheep and Goat Rearing in Ecologically Fragile Zone, GOI, Ministry of Agriculture, Department of Agriculture and Cooperation, New Delhi.

IWWI (2003): 'Poverty-Focused Smallholder Water Management-Promoting Innovative Water Harvesting and Irrigation Systems to Support Sustainable Livelihoods in South Asia', Project completion and Synthesis Report, IWMI, Hyderabad.

Mainuddin, M. (2002): pers comm. (-2000): Groundwater Irrigation in Bangladesh: 'Tool for Poverty Alleviation' or 'Cause of Mass Poisoning'? Proceedings of the Symposium on Intensive Use of Groundwater; Challenges and Opportunities, December 10-14, Valencia, Spain.

Managurkar, B.R. and C Ravi Kumar (2001): 'Livestock-Environment Interactions in Watersheds in India', CALPI/ SDC, New Delhi.

Mishra, Sudhakar (2004): 'Alternative Institutions for Electricity Retailing: Assessment of Orissa Experiments'. Anand, IWMI-Tata Water Policy Programme (upublished repot).

Moench, M., J. Burke and Y. Monjech (2002): Rethinking the approach to groundwater and food security, Food and Agriculture Organisation of Mukherji, A. and A. Kishore (2003): Tubewell Transfer in Gujarat: A Study of the GWRDC Approach, Colombo, Sri Lanka. IWMI Research Report No. 69.

NCAER (1999): 'Economic and Environmental Benefits of Watershed-Based Dry Land Development Progrmmes in India' in Anil Agarwal (ed), *The Challenge of the Balance*, Centre for Science and Environment, New Delhi.

Prasad, D. (et al) (1984): 'Resource, Poverty and Technology: Enterprise choice by Small Farmers', field report (mimeo), IRMA, Anand.

Ramana, R. (1991): 'Watershed Approach to Dryland Agricultural Development;, *Indian Journal of Agricultural Economics*, No. 3, July-September.

Rao, Hanumantha C. H. (2000): 'Watershed Development in India: Recent Experiences and Emerging Issues', *Economic and Political Weekly*, November 4, pp 3943-47.

Shankar, Kripa (1982): 'Working of State Tubewells in Phulpur Block of Allahabad District' G.B. Pant Institute of Social Sciences, Allahabad (mimeo).

Shah, T. and K.V. Raju (1897a): 'Working of Groundwater Markets in Andhara Pradesh and Gujarat: Results of Two Village Studies', *Economic and Political Weekly,* March 26, A23-A28.

Singh, D.R. and R.P. Singh (2003): 'Groundwater Markets and Issues of Equity and Reliability to Water Access: A Case of Watern Uttar Pradesh, *Indian Journal of a Agricultural Economics,* January– March 1 (58).

Shah, T., B.V. Koppen, D. Merrey, M.D. Lange, M. Samad (2002): 'Institutional Alternatives in African Samllholder Irrigation: Lessons from International Experience with Irrigation Management Transfer', Colombo, Sri Lanka, IWMI, V,24 p (IWMI research report 60).

United Nations (2000): 'Perspectives on Integrated Basin Management for a Policy Study on the Huaihe River Basin, China', The United Nations, New York.

Vermillion, Douglas (eds) (1996): 'The Privatisation and Self-Management of Irrigation: Final Report No. 70, Colombo, Sri Lanka.

Wang, J., and J. Huang (2002) 'Tubewell Management Technical Efficiency (in Chinese)', *Journal of Water Resources Advances,* Vol. 2.

Zhang, Lubio (2004): 'The Economics of Electricity Supply to Tubewell Irrigation in North China', IWMI-Tata Water Policy Programme (draft report), Anand, India.

Zhang, L. and H.U. Dinghuan (2003): 'Sustaining Water User Associations: Problems and Policies', Unpublished report for Public Policy Programme of the Ford Foundation, Beijing.

Index

■■■